LUKE'S STORY OF JESUS

LUKE'S STORY OF JESUS

O. C. Edwards, Jr.

FORTRESS PRESS   PHILADELPHIA

Library of Congress Cataloging in Publication Data

Edwards, O. C. (Otis Carl), 1928–
  Luke's story of Jesus.

  Companion to: Mark's story of Jesus / by Werner H. Kelber. 1979.
  1. Jesus Christ—History of doctrines—Early church, ca. 30-600. 2. Bible. N.T. Luke—Criticism, interpretation, etc. I. Title.
BT198.E32   226′.406   81–43076
ISBN 0-8006-1611-1   AACR2

9008C81   Printed in the United States of America   1–1611

*Dedicated to
the pastor of
St. Luke's United Methodist Church
New Orleans, Louisiana
The Reverend Conrad Paul Edwards
with the love and respect
of his brother*

Contents

Preface

This volume is part of a plan; it was written to be a companion to *Mark's Story of Jesus* by Werner H. Kelber (Philadelphia: Fortress Press, 1979). Like Kelber's book, this one grew out of a course for lay theological education which was taught at the Seabury Academy of Seabury-Western Theological Seminary. The present form of this book owes much to the members of that class, and it would be improper to overlook my indebtedness to them.

Like Kelber's book, this one is intended for an audience without technical background in New Testament study, and thus footnotes and scholarly language are avoided. Until recently there has been a scholarly consensus on how Luke should be interpreted, and since the present work departs from the consensus, it seems only fair to indicate where that is so. I have tried to do that without imposing on the reader a confusing list of authors and titles.

Since bibliographic references will not be made elsewhere, some admission of my own indebtedness and some indication of where the reader can go for further study is appropriate. The prevailing consensus, from which I have learned most of what I know about Luke and from which I have only recently departed, was developed by Hans Conzelmann in *The Theology of St. Luke* (New York: Harper & Row, 1961). Recent studies from which I have profited include Jacob Jervell, *Luke and the People of God* (Minneapolis: Augsburg Publishing House, 1972); Luke T. Johnson, *The Literary Function of Possessions in Luke–Acts* (Missoula: Scholars Press, 1977); and David L. Tiede, *Prophecy and History in Luke–Acts* (Philadelphia: Fortress Press, 1980). John Drury is another scholar to whom I am indebted, particularly for his small popular commentary on Luke (*Luke: A Commentary on the New Testament in Modern English* [New York: Macmillan Co., 1973]). The influence of Raymond E. Brown, *The Birth of the Messiah*

(New York: Doubleday & Co., 1977), on the early sections of this work will be recognized by those familiar with that book. I have turned often to my colleague Richard Pervo for information and advice. None of these authorities is to be held responsible for any lapses of scholarly vision in these pages.

One stylistic point needs to be made. It is common to refer to both a gospel and its author by the same name. Doing so can be confusing, since Luke or Mark can be the antecedent for "he" in one sentence and for "it" in another. Further complication arises if one asks whether the gospels were written by apostles or their companions called Matthew, Mark, Luke, and John. Most modern scholars question such attributions of authorship. I am willing to pass on that question in relation to Luke. All I mean by "Luke" is either the gospel or its author, without presupposing anything more about the identity of the author than that he wrote the gospel that bears his name.

Introduction

A gospel can be studied in many ways: it can be read devotion-ally; it can be examined for the contribution it makes to our knowledge of the life of Jesus; it can be looked at to see what use it makes of stories about Jesus and sayings attributed to him that were already in existence when the gospel was written; it can be studied for its literary patterns or for the way that its religious practices and ideas resemble those of other ancient oriental or Greco-Roman peoples.

Our method will be to see how the way that one gospel writer tells his story is related to the interpretation of Jesus that he wishes to share through that story. To say this is to state what should be one of the most obvious truths about a gospel. A gospel is not just a story. It is not even just a biography of Jesus in the sense that it is told to satisfy our curiosity about Jesus. No, a gospel is written to bring people to belief in Jesus. This point is made clearly in John 20:30–31: "Now Jesus did many other signs in the presence of the disciples, which are not written in this book; but these are written that you may believe that Jesus is the Christ, the Son of God, and that believing you may have life in his name."

A gospel is written to tell the story of Jesus in a way that will bring the reader to a conclusion about Jesus, a conclusion upon which the reader will act. One way of saying this is that the gospels are tools of evangelism (not very surprising, since our word "evangelism" is derived from the Greek word that we translate "gospel," *evangelion*). Another way of saying it is that the gospels communicate theology through narrative rather than through abstract reasoning.

To say that Luke's gospel will be studied to see how he com-municates theology through his narrative indicates several charac-teristics of the appropriate method of study. For example, single passages cannot be examined in isolation from the rest of the

11

gospel; each story must be seen as a part of a whole. People who are familiar with gospel stories from hearing them read in church usually know them as individual stories rather than as constituents of a continuous narrative, since they have heard the stories read one at a time as the gospel lection for a particular day. This means that a single story is seldom related to its context in a gospel and thus its relation to what goes before or comes after is missed.

Further, even though most churches now have a three-year lectionary cycle in which most of the gospel readings for a particular year come from the same gospel, it is still easy to run together the versions of the same story that appear in the different gospels and unconsciously transfer to one account details from another. This process could be called unconscious harmonization, and the impression left is that there is only one gospel, not four. Then it becomes impossible to detect the point about Jesus that the writer was trying to make by telling the story the way he did. Therefore at one stage it becomes necessary to filter from the memory all the details from accounts in Matthew or Mark that parallel a story under study in Luke; there is no other way to be sure that one sees the point Luke was trying to make by the way that *he* told the story. Treating each of the four accounts as unique is the only way to avoid acting as though there were but one. The church has kept four gospels because it prizes the nuances that each has and does not want any individual flavors to be lost in some great gospel stew.

Even though all the details of other versions must be filtered from the memory at one stage of study, there is another stage at which conscious comparison is useful. Most New Testament scholars believe that when Luke wrote he had open before him a copy of Mark, and that he also had access to a collection of other material about Jesus, mostly sayings (usually identified as the Q source), that Matthew also used. This means that one way to learn the special meaning conveyed by Luke's version of a story is to see what use he made of his sources. The technique for doing that with Mark is different from the one used with the sayings source. Since Mark was itself a source for Luke, any change can be ascribed to Luke. Because we do not have the sayings source in its original form, however, but only postulate its existence because so much such similar material appears in Matthew and Luke, a difference between the two does not necessarily tell us which form was original or even that either was. For that reason, the indication of special Lukan emphases that the alteration of a source gives will be much more obvious from a comparison of Luke with Mark than from a similar comparison with Matthew. While this book is about the theology that was communicated through Luke's narration of the story of Jesus, and will concentrate on that narration, clarification will be sought occasionally through a side look at Mark and less often from a glance at Matthew.

John will hardly enter the discussion, because it does not use Mark or the sayings material as a source. It derives from a different stream of tradition about Jesus. Since Matthew and Luke do use the same sources, they can be printed in parallel columns with Mark to facilitate comparisons and contrasts. When they are printed like that, they can be seen together (Greek: *synoptikos*); thus Matthew, Mark, and Luke are called the synoptic gospels. Volumes in which they are so printed are variously called synopses, gospel harmonies, or gospel parallels. These make valuable tools, since they enable one to see readily what is unique to one gospel and what is shared with others.

In this contrasting of the way that Luke tells the story of Jesus with the way that other gospel writers do, the purpose is not like that of a trial lawyer comparing the testimony of a number of witnesses to find out what actually happened. By and large, such historical considerations will be put aside in favor of theological ones. The constant question, then, will be not whether what Luke said was an accurate historical record of an event but rather what point he was making about Jesus by telling that story the way he did.

It would be possible at this time to say something about when Luke was written and under what circumstances. Since, however, any evidence about such questions comes from the text of the gospel itself, since scholars have been able to reach few agreements about the meaning of that evidence, and since the purpose of this book is to interpret the story line of the gospel rather than to make historical reconstructions, such questions can be put aside for the moment and resurrected only as they bear upon some issue under discussion.

In sum, the meaning of Luke is best learned from the text of Luke. When that is realized, further delay is pointless.

1

The Long-awaited Birth

LUKE 1:1—2:52

A BOOK WITH A PREFACE

This gospel is not the only book in the New Testament written by the author called Luke. The Acts of the Apostles, a history of how the Christian movement expanded from Jerusalem to Rome under the impetus of the Holy Spirit, was also written by Luke and was originally read together with the gospel as a two-volume work. Very often things that are not clear in the gospel make perfect sense when they are understood in the perspective of the completion of Luke's presentation in Acts. Luke's two volumes are the only books in the New Testament that begin with a preface like that of some Greco-Roman literary works. From this it is apparent that Luke was familiar with such a convention and thus wished to have his work understood not just as a sectarian writing from a minority culture within the Roman Empire but also as something worthy of the attention of the book-reading public.

Luke dedicates his books to a man he calls "most excellent Theophilus." The honorific address of "most excellent" was used at the time for high Roman officials, but since we know nothing of Theophilus beyond what we learn in Luke's two prefaces, we do not know if such office was his title to such respectful address. It has been suggested that Theophilus was a judge or some other dignitary who could help Christians brought before Roman courts, but Luke's two books have much more religion than legal defense. Would such an official have bothered to read all that? If, on the other hand, Theophilus was being catechized in the Christian faith, it is obvious that Luke intended for others to profit from his book as well; these are public rather than private documents. While the name Theophilus means ''God-lover,'' its use is probably not symbolic. Theophilus was probably Luke's patron, and therefore a real person.

The literary form of address and the religious content suggest that Luke wrote for a double audience: for literate Greco-Roman people who might be interested in Christianity and for Christians in need of reinforcement for their beliefs.

Some have seen this preface as an indication that Luke wished his work to be understood as a historical writing. Comparison is made to the preface that a contemporary of Luke, the Jewish historian Josephus, wrote to his work *Against Apion:*

> In my history of our *Antiquities*, most excellent Epaphroditus, I have, I think, made sufficiently clear . . . the extreme antiquity of our Jewish race. . . . Since, however, I observe that a considerable number of persons . . . discredit my history, I consider it my duty to devote a brief treatise to all these points . . . to instruct all who desire to know the truth concerning the antiquity of our race. As witnesses to my statements I propose to call the writers who, in the estimation of the Greeks, are the most trustworthy authorities on antiquity as a whole. (1.1–4)

It is easy for the contemporary reader and scholar to apply to this idea of historical writing the standards of verification that were set in the nineteenth century by Leopold von Ranke; history in our sense is a modern invention! Against this notion it should be said that similar prefaces were used in the historical romances that were being written in Luke's time. The existence of a preface proves nothing by itself. When we look at Luke's writing we discover not only that he made historical mistakes (e.g., about the census under Quirinius in 2:2), but also that he probably created some of his stories for their theological effect, as will become obvious in the discussion of the infancy narratives that follows. It would be anachronistic to imagine that Luke could have written history in the modern technical sense, and unfair to judge his work by criteria for accuracy that were not developed until many centuries after his time.

Luke did not mean modern historiography when he said that he would write an ''orderly account'' based on tradition that had been "delivered" by "those who from the beginning were eyewitnesses and ministers of the word," and what he did mean can only become apparent from a study of the text he produced. From time to time in what follows there will be reference to some of these terms from the preface, and an effort will be made to supply them with specific content.

A DIPTYCH OF ANNUNCIATIONS

Many readers of the gospels are so accustomed to harmonizing them unconsciously that it may never have occurred to them that there is anything remarkable about Luke's beginning his story of Jesus with tales about his infancy. Yet Mark, on whom Luke and Matthew depend, began his story with Jesus' baptism as an adult by John the Baptist. John, representing a different strand of tradition about Jesus, began his gospel with a poetic theological prologue which he followed with an account of John the Baptist's witness to Jesus. Another theory is that the author of John began with the witness of the Baptist, and a later editor added the poetic prologue. The story of the miracle at Cana in the second chapter of John can be considered an example of the kind of revelation about the "hidden life" of Jesus between his birth and ministry that Luke's story of Jesus in the Temple at age twelve is, but otherwise John confines his account to the period of Jesus' ministry.

Only Matthew joins Luke in telling of the earliest days of Jesus on earth. Both evangelists wrote at a time when Jesus' status was thought to have become apparent at his conception. Originally that recognition was thought to have occurred at the resurrection, but afterwards it had been moved up to his baptism. Now it was being focused on the conception. Very soon, in the prologue to John, it will be seen that Jesus must have existed eternally with the Father before the creation of the world.

There are many points about Jesus' earliest days upon which Luke and Matthew agree. While this book is concerned only with Luke, it is useful to recognize these agreements, since they suggest that the information in question did not originate with Luke but came from tradition on which Matthew also drew. Both evangelists place Jesus' birth during the reign of Herod the Great (d. 4 B.C.). They agree that he was born at Bethlehem and grew up at

Nazareth, that his mother was Mary, who conceived him virginally by the power of the Holy Spirit, and that her husband was a descendant of David named Joseph. Both also relate that the baby was given the name Jesus because of a divine command relayed through an angel.

This is where the resemblance ends. Luke's story focuses on Mary, and Matthew's on Joseph. One example of such focus: the angelic annunciation is made to Mary in Luke and to Joseph in Matthew. Only Matthew tells of Joseph's reaction to learning that his fiancée was pregnant. The visitors who view the newborn child are shepherds in Luke, while in Matthew they are eastern astrologers, Magi—from the same root as "magic." Luke understands Nazareth to have been the hometown of Mary and Joseph before Jesus' birth, but Matt. 2:22–23 seems to indicate that they did not move there until after the sojourn in Egypt—which Luke not only fails to mention but seems to exclude in 2:39. Notice that some of these statements are merely inconsistent with one another, while others are mutually contradictory. Mutually exclusive claims cannot both be true in the same way, and we must deal with the possibility that the truth of some of the infancy narratives may be theological rather than historical.

Another difference between Luke and Matthew is that Luke parallels his accounts of the annunciation about Jesus and the birth of Jesus with stories of the annunciation and birth of John the Baptist, while Matthew does not. Furthermore, the two annunciation stories in Luke follow a pattern that has become familiar from the stories of the births of such Old Testament worthies as Ishmael (Gen. 16:7–12), Isaac (Gen. 17:1–21), and Samson (Judg. 13:3–25). There are five steps to the pattern:

1. An angel appears to the person to whom the announcement is to be made.

2. That person experiences fear in the presence of the supernatural visitor.

3. In delivering the message—
   a. The angel calls the recipient by name.
   b. In the address the angel refers to some quality of the recipient.

c. The recipient is told not to be afraid.

d. A woman is or is about to become pregnant.

e. She will give birth to the (male) child.

f. The name by which the child is to be called is given.

g. The meaning of the name is explained.

h. Something is said about what the child will grow up to do.

4. The recipient either asks how that can happen or asks for a sign.

5. A sign is given that reassures the recipient.

A quick check shows that all these steps occur in both the annunciation to Zechariah, the father of John the Baptist, and the annunciation to Mary. As will become apparent, it is the very similarities of the two stories that make the differences between them—and therefore between the two persons whose births they announce—the more obvious. Because these two annunciation stories and the two birth stories are so obviously written to be compared with one another, scholars have referred to them as *diptychs*, pairs of portraits that are hinged together.

The reader of Luke in its original Greek senses a literary shift in moving from the preface into the annunciation story about John the Baptist. The preface exhibits classical Greek style not only in its form but also in its grammar and vocabulary, while the account of the annunciation to Zechariah and most of the other infancy narratives reflect the Semitic sort of Greek that is used in the Septuagint (LXX), the Greek translation of the Old Testament. Not just the language but all the aspects of these stories are redolent of the odor of Jewish sanctity; for Luke there is more continuity than discontinuity between the old and new covenants. There is no necessary inconsistency between them; only the hardness of the hearts of the religious leaders forced Christians to separate from the Temple. Nevertheless, the relation between the covenants is one of promise and fulfillment. For that reason, *one of the most consistent Lukan themes is the fulfillment of prophecy*. It may also be observed here parenthetically that Luke is a skilled master of Greek prose who can fit his style to his subject or characters.

The Temple piety of John's parents appears in their priestly descent and in their names: Zechariah is the name of the prophet whose book precedes that of Malachi, in which promise is given of a prophet like Elijah (Mal. 4:5), and Elizabeth was the name of the wife of Aaron, the ancestor of the priestly tribe. Although she and Zechariah were punctilious in their religious duties, Elizabeth, like many of the famous mothers of the Old Testament (especially Abraham's wife Sarah, and Hannah the mother of Samuel), had been barren for many years. Most priests had the honor of offering the incense only once in their lives. Luke's information about Temple ritual is accurate here, although he makes some mistakes in other places. This has led some to conclude that he was a gentile convert to Judaism before he became a Christian, and thus had a literary rather than a practical knowledge of such matters.

It is important to note that the first word of the good news of the salvation God was preparing for his people is announced in the Temple. Then, too, the son that will be born will be a Nazarite like Samson and Samuel, neither having his hair cut nor drinking wine (Num. 6:1–21). "He will be filled with the Holy Spirit even from his mother's womb" and, as Mal. 4:6 says Elijah will do, he will turn parents and children toward one another. Zechariah's response to this announcement is taken by Gabriel to express a lack of faith, so the sign that is given him is that he will be mute until after all the prophecy is fulfilled.

Like the announcement of the birth of John the Baptist to Zechariah, the announcement of the birth of Jesus to Mary also has all five ingredients of an Old Testament annunciation story: (1) appearance of the angel, (2) the fear of the recipient, (3) the message, (4) the objection or request for a sign, and (5) the sign. Because these two annunciation stories parallel one another so closely in form, it is easy to notice the differences between them and thus to learn about the differences in the status of the two children. Essentially, there are three such differences:

1. John the Baptist is described only as *great before the Lord*; Jesus is called great absolutely and without qualification.

2. John was to be *filled with the Holy Spirit even from his mother's womb*, but the Holy Spirit would enable Mary to conceive Jesus without a human father—or a divine one either, because the Holy Spirit is not thought of in any way as inseminating Mary.

3. John's mission was to *make ready for the Lord a people prepared*, while Jesus was to receive *the throne of his father David* so that he would reign over Israel forever.

The degree of miracle involved in a virginal conception is much greater than that involved in conception by a barren woman as a result of intercourse with her husband. Perhaps, too, the superiority of Jesus is indicated in the superior response that his parent makes to the announcement that he will be born. John's father is said not to have believed the words of the angel, but Mary's response was: "Behold, I am the handmaid [slave] of the Lord; let it be to me according to your word." Since Mary has such complete faith, it may be wondered why she asked how she could have a child without having sexual intercourse (the meaning of the Old Testament expression "to know a man"). The first reason is that an objection or a request for a sign is one of the ingredients of an annunciation story, and the second is that she asks for the reader's benefit, that is, Luke has her ask so that the angel's response can inform the reader.

Since the traditional Hail Mary is based on this story and the next one, it is worth asking whether Luke thought of Mary as "full of grace." If he did, it was not because of merit she had before the conception, merit that caused God to deem her worthy of being the mother of his Son. It was rather because of the conception itself that she could be considered "full of grace" or "highly favored." Mary was not the source of any merit; she had only what was imputed to her by the Father.

The annunciation story closes with the departure of the angel from Mary. Explicit notice of someone's departure is the way that Luke closes most of the scenes in his infancy narratives.

In the story of Mary's visitation to Elizabeth (1:39–56) the two parties that had been held apart in the diptych are brought together. Elizabeth was Mary's relative, and Mary was the first person to be informed of her pregnancy. She was informed not by Elizabeth, however, but by the angel who revealed it to her miraculously (1:36). The narrative necessity behind Elizabeth's hiding herself for five months, as mentioned in 1:24, was so that Mary would be the first to know. It was the knowledge that her kinswoman was also to be involved in giving birth miraculously that motivated

Mary to travel the considerable distance from Nazareth to the Judean hills.

When she arrived, the fetal John the Baptist in Elizabeth's uterus jumped in obeisance to his Messiah cousin now in Mary's womb. Note that Mary was a virgin when the announcement came to her and that she "arose and went with haste" to see Elizabeth. Although she and Joseph had taken the first step of Jewish marriage, that of exchanging vows in the presence of witnesses, they had not yet taken the second step, in which the bride moved to the home of the groom. Mary's going with haste to see Elizabeth leaves no time for that move between the annunciation and the visitation. Thus the conception was as Luke says it was, virginal. The worshipful intrauterine movement of John reiterates the point of the diptych, John's subordination to Jesus. That theme is then made explicit in Elizabeth's Old Testament (Judg. 5:4; Jth. 13:18) description of Mary as "blessed among women" because the fruit of her womb is blessed. Mary is the mother of Elizabeth's Lord.

Even though the visitation scene underlines the point of the diptych, some scholars have felt that it disrupts the balance achieved between the two annunciations. They are reinforced in that feeling by manuscript variations as to whether Mary or Elizabeth recited the Magnificat (1:46–55) and by the inappropriateness of much of the content of this canticle to either of them. The major theme of the hymn is the reversal of fortunes that results from God's promised mercy to his people. Only verse 48 sounds particularly suited to Mary. For that reason, some scholars think the Magnificat was a hymn borrowed by Luke from a community of Jewish Christians and revised slightly for use here. They go so far as to say it may not have been in his first draft and was instead inserted at a later time. In any case, the hymn puts Mary and Elizabeth in the framework of Jewish piety as it looked forward to the birth of the Messiah. Luke's sense of the two covenants is expressed again.

THE TWOFOLD NATIVITY

The birth of John the Baptist is set with the birth of Jesus in another diptych arrangement. After the infancy stories, however, the ministries of John and Jesus are not set down side by side but rather are presented end to end; John's ministry is over before Jesus' begins. That end-to-end arrangement has caused some scholars to speculate that John and Jesus belong to different ages. The appearance of the two figures side by side in the infancy narratives undercuts that argument. Other scholars have tried to postulate a source for the material about John in the infancy narratives. They have deduced from various New Testament passages (Luke 7:18–35; Acts 19:1–7; John 3:22—4:3) that John had his own disciples and community and that this community preserved the traditions about him that were the source from which Luke drew this material about John. It seems likely, however, that for his purposes Luke assembled the material out of what was known about John from the body of the gospel and from the pattern of the annunciation story.

The hints that John may have had his own disciples who never became followers of Jesus raise questions about the degree to which he understood himself as the forerunner of Jesus and especially about how correct Luke was in treating him as a relative of Jesus. The most that one can be certain about is that Jesus was baptized by John; perhaps John understood himself as preparing the way for the Father rather than for the Son.

This diptych is not as well balanced as the other. John's birth is narrated quickly, and the rest of the space is taken up by marvelous events that accompanied his circumcision and naming. The setting for Jesus' birth and the miracles that surround it do take some time to relate. By the same token, the Nunc Dimittis, the canticle in 2:29–32 that follows Jesus' presentation in the Temple, is much shorter than the Benedictus, the canticle in 1:68–79 that comes after the Baptist's circumcision. The report of Jesus' circumcision is only one verse long (2:21).

Because Elizabeth had been hidden, her "neighbors and kinsfolk" had not known that she was pregnant and that God had taken away what was considered to be the curse of her barrenness. During the Old Testament period there was little belief in life after death, and people hoped to live on in the lives of their children as a way of achieving immortality. For that reason, childlessness was thought to be the ultimate tragedy and disgrace. Thus Elizabeth could say when she became pregnant that God had taken away her reproach (1:25).

The family and friends gathered for the baby's circumcision when he was eight days old, in accordance with the Torah (Lev. 12:3). They tried to name the boy after his father, but Elizabeth objected and called for him to be named John. Her doing so was miraculous, because Zechariah had been rendered speechless after the annunciation in which he was commanded to call the baby by that name, and thus had not been able to communicate to his wife what the angel had said. Shocked by Elizabeth's departure from custom, the relatives asked the father by signs to name the child. Even though he could not hear what his wife had said, he astonished the bystanders by writing on a wax tablet the very name that she had wanted their child to have. By then the prophecy of the angel had been fulfilled, and so Zechariah's speech returned to him, a new occasion for wonder to all who were present. Religious awe in the presence of a supernatural event is a reaction to which Luke often calls attention. The people who heard about these events "laid them up in their hearts," a practice that Mary will keep under similar circumstances (2:19, 51).

The Benedictus, which appears to be tacked on to the end of the story, resembles the Magnificat in a number of ways, not the least of which is the irrelevance of its content to the occasion except for a couple of verses (1:76–77). If scholars are correct that the Magnificat is a Jewish-Christian hymn that Luke adapted for inclusion in his gospel, then the Benedictus could well be another such hymn. In such a case, however, the borrowed material would have been added because the author thought its inclusion made his story richer. Thus the question of whether Luke wrote these hymns himself or borrowed them from someone else is irrelevant to the question of what he intended to communicate through the stories that contain them.

The section ends with the information that "the child grew and became strong, filled with wisdom," a report similar to others that are made about Jesus (2:40, 52). It is also said that John "was in the wilderness [desert] till the day of his manifestation to Israel," a smooth transition that gets John offstage until his ministry but that already places him on the spot where he will next appear.

In dating the birth of Jesus in relation to the census under
Quirinius, Luke is almost certainly incorrect. He and Matthew are
agreed that Jesus was born during the lifetime of Herod the Great,
who died in 4 B.C. The census under Quirinius did not occur until
A.D. 6. Far from being worldwide, or even reaching to Galilee
where Nazareth is located, it was confined to Judea because that
was all the territory over which Quirinius had authority. And we
know of no Roman census that required people to go to their
ancestral city for registration. Nor can we imagine that there were
a number of censuses under Quirinius or anyone else, because the
Jews hated them and there was actually a revolt at the time of the
one under Quirinius. By the same token, Luke's knowledge of
Jewish marital customs must have been faulty; the transition from
the engaged to the married state is accomplished by the bride's
moving into the groom's home, something that Mary must have
already done if she traveled with Joseph to Bethlehem. Thus it is
inappropriate to continue to refer to her as engaged (2:5).

Luke must have been under the impression that Mary and
Joseph were originally from Nazareth even though he knew that
Jesus was born in Bethlehem. The census furnishes a motivation
for the trip. It also allows Luke to set the birth of Jesus in the
context of world history by telling who was ruler where at the time.
The uncertainty about whether the trip occurred for the census
creates uncertainty about where they lodged or did not lodge,
although, as one scholar has said, "Luke seems more interested in
telling his audience where Mary laid the newborn baby" than in
reporting the birth.

It was very important for the baby to be born in Bethlehem, the
city of David, the shepherd king. On the basis of Mic. 5:2 there was
a widespread expectation at the time that the messiah would be
born there. All this reinforces the picture of Jesus as the royal heir
of David. And in the city of the shepherd king, what would be more
natural than that the newborn babe be visited by shepherds to
whom angels had announced the marvelous birth? This annunciation to the shepherds echoes Isa. 9:6: "For to us a child is born, to
us a son is given." As a result of the visit, we hear again of the
religious awe that greeted the reports. We would seriously mis-
diagnose the nature of this story if we asked if any of those who

heard this report later became followers of Jesus. What we have is a scene of supernatural revelation before which the reader should imitate the shepherds and gaze in worshipful wonder. Mary also "kept all these things, pondering them in her heart." By so doing, she served as many Lukan characters do in furnishing an example for the response of the reader.

As noted above, the circumcision and naming of Jesus were disposed of with one verse instead of being made the core of a series of marvelous events as in the case of John the Baptist. Instead, such events cluster around the presentation of Jesus in the Temple (2:22–40). The report of the presentation furnishes additional evidence that Luke was a non-Palestinian convert to Judaism, because he treats other matters of Jewish law the way that someone acquainted with literature would rather than one with firsthand knowledge. "Every male that opens the womb shall be called holy to the Lord" is not an exact quotation, but combines elements from Exod. 13:2, 12, and 15. The original reference was to the Passover when the firstborn Israelites were preserved by God; because of their preservation, they and their successors belonged to him. This belonging to the Lord was understood at first as serving him liturgically, but when the tribe of Levi took over all priestly duty, firstborn sons from other tribes could be redeemed by an offering. The offering mentioned in 2:24, however, is for the purification of a poor woman after childbirth (Lev. 12:8). Luke speaks of the purification of both parents, while it was only the mother who was purified. Note too that delivery rather than conception was thought to be ritually defiling. It is doubtful that mothers still went to the Temple for this purification during Jesus' time. Much of Luke's inspiration for this story must have come from the account of the presentation of the infant Samuel in the Temple (1 Sam. 1:24–28).

Mary and Joseph obey the Law in bringing Jesus to the Temple. At the Temple they meet two prophets. The major elements of Jewish piety are brought together in this combination of law, prophets, and Temple. Simeon and Anna represent this piety in the special form of the *Anawim*, the poor, who understood themselves as the faithful remnant of Israel who were looking for the "consolation of Israel," the messiah. It was from such a group who had become Christians that some scholars believe that Luke borrowed the canticles in the infancy narrative, such as the Nunc Dimittis that Simeon says when he takes the infant Jesus into his arms (2:29–32). Since he sees Jesus as "a light for revelation to the Gentiles," he gives to the Lukan birth stories the universal dimension that the Magi give to those in Matthew, although because Luke has all of Acts in which to discuss the gentile mission, he does not read it back into the ministry of Jesus as Matthew and Mark do.

After this discharge of the duties of the Torah there is an easy transition back to Nazareth. It should be noted, however, that Luke excludes the possibility of a journey into Egypt such as Matthew describes.

Most religions have stories about the childhood years of their founders, and such stories abound for other people of notable accomplishment as well. There is a human inclination to see later achievement forecast in childhood behavior. While Christianity produced a number of apocryphal gospels that contain such stories about Jesus, mostly unedifying, Luke's account of Jesus' visit to the Temple at the age of twelve (2:41–52) is the only "hidden-life" story in the canonical gospels, unless, as suggested above, John's story of the wedding at Cana is meant to be of that variety.

There were three pilgrim feasts for which Jews were expected to go to the Temple in Jerusalem: Passover and Unleavened Bread, Weeks or Pentecost, and Tabernacles (Exod. 23:17; 34:23). But in the time of Jesus many of the Jews living outside Palestine in what was called the Dispersion made only one such pilgrimage in their lifetime, and those from within the country may have attended only one feast a year.

Nothing will impede the understanding of this story so much as taking it as literal historical truth in every detail and then trying to understand what happened psychologically. We do not really need to ask why Joseph and Mary got through a day's journey, a twenty-mile walk, without noticing that their child was missing. The explanation is literary and theological: He had to be missing for the story to happen and the display of his unusual nature to occur. In the Temple, Jesus was seen to belong to God rather than to Joseph and Mary. Yet he was willing because of their lack of understanding to return home with them and submit himself to

them until the time came for his revelation. Thus this one manifestation of his true nature in his childhood accounts for there being no
other such manifestations. It also documents the claim for his
wisdom made in verses 40 and 52.

A point also needs to be made about Mary's misunderstanding.
How can she be surprised by the unusual nature of her son after the
annunciation, the visitation, the homage of the shepherds who had
received an angelic revelation, and the prophecies of Simeon and
Anna? Was she Our Lady of Invincible Ignorance? No. Part of the
answer lies in the Lukan prose style, which creates individual
edifying scenes without asking how consistent they are with one
another. Part of it lies in Mary's role as the only person who is a
faithful member of the household of God in (a) the infancy, (b) the
ministry of Jesus, and (c) the postresurrection community (Acts
1:14). In order to act appropriately at each stage, she cannot carry
over too much insight from previous stages.

2
Jesus' Ministry in Galilee

LUKE 3:1—9:50

CREDENTIALS FOR MINISTRY

If the infancy stories were eliminated, Luke's gospel could be divided naturally into three sections of almost equal length. The first deals with Jesus' ministry in the area around the lake of Galilee, the second is an episodic account of his journey up to Jerusalem (9:51—19:27), and the third tells of his teaching, arrest, crucifixion, and resurrection in Jerusalem (19:28—24:53). The transition from the infancy narratives to the ministry in Galilee is accomplished by a series of events that show Jesus' qualifications for the ministry he is about to begin: the activity of John the Baptist as messianic herald, Jesus' reception of the Holy Spirit at the time of his baptism, and his successful resistance of the temptations of Satan. There is also interjected into this sequence Jesus' genealogical chart, which documents his descent from David and is therefore a messianic credential of prime importance.

The beginning of the ministry of John the Baptist, the messianic herald, is solemnly marked by a complex dating that begins with the Roman emperor's year of reign and includes the names of Roman governors and client kings in Israel and surrounding territory, and the names of the high priests at Jerusalem. This method of dating was standard before the introduction of a universal calendar with B.C./A.D. dates. Greco-Roman historians, for instance, often began their works with such chronological data. The effect here is so impressive that some scholars have decided this must

29

have been the original beginning of the book, the infancy narratives
having been added later. That argument is not so effective as it
sounds at first, because the person responsible for the final form of
the gospel did not think this solemn dating was inappropriate for a
transitional chapter; if he had, he could have changed it. What is
good enough for the final form ought to be good enough for the first
draft. The date, incidentally, falls between A.D. 27 and A.D. 29. The
real point of the date is not to tell when John's ministry began but to
mark the beginning of John's witness to Jesus. In the account of the
ministry, as in the infancy narratives, the only significance of John
the Baptist is that he was the forerunner of Jesus.

The message of John the Baptist, according to Luke, was a
"baptism of repentance for the remission of sins," the message
assigned to him by Mark. Matthew depicts John as also proclaim-
ing the near approach of the kingdom of heaven. In order to
interpret Luke correctly, one needs to repress any curiosity about
what John really taught. Luke saw him exclusively as the one who
"prepared the way of the Lord." Thus the baptism that John
administered, and any other activity in which he engaged, is not
assigned independent significance by Luke. A contrast is drawn,
however, between John's baptism and that of Jesus: John's was
with water only, while Jesus would baptize "with the Holy Spirit
and with fire." Jesus' baptism with fire and the Holy Spirit alludes
to Pentecost (Acts 2:1–4). In this as in all things, Luke makes John
the Baptist's subordination to Jesus explicit.

In 3:7 Luke identifies those who came out to hear John as "the
multitudes." In the parallel passage in Matthew (3:7) the audience
of John is described as "Pharisees and Sadducees." Luke's more
inclusive term allows him to lengthen his presentation of the message of the Baptist by adding ethical instruction to tax collectors
and soldiers, social groups that would have been excluded from
membership in the two religious parties.

The event reported in Luke 3:21–22 is traditionally referred to as
the "baptism" of Jesus, and certainly that occurrence is alluded
to, but even in the earlier form of the story in Mark the emphasis
was already on something else, Jesus' reception of the Holy Spirit
and heavenly vision. In the Greek of Luke, however, the baptism is
relegated to a participial phrase setting the baptism of Jesus in the
context of all the other baptisms that John performed. Characteris-

tically, Luke also made note of Jesus' praying at the time. In this incidental reference to the baptizing activity of John, the subordination of the Baptist to Jesus reaches its nadir, and John disappears from the scene.

Luke and Matthew both treat Jesus' heavenly vision at the time of his baptism as more objective than it appears in Mark. The full extent of the subjectivity of the Markan narrative is obvious only in Greek, but it should not be overestimated: Mark did not have a twentieth-century psychological point of view that regarded visions as hallucinations. For him what happened was "real," but only Jesus, with his privileged access to the heavenly world, was aware of it.

Luke's account of the descent of the Spirit is crucial for his understanding of the identity and status of Jesus, but it does not delineate his full understanding. Jesus, who had been conceived through the Holy Spirit, now receives the Spirit. While the Spirit had been given sporadically in the past and would become the essence of the life of the church in Acts, it—we are not yet to a trinitarian he—would be Jesus' unique possession for his ministry. In spite of the fact that some manuscripts have the voice from heaven quote Ps. 2:7 here, "You are my son, today I have begotten you," this is not the beginning of Jesus' identity as the Spirit-begotten; Luke clearly dates that at the conception. Yet what happens here is real and significant, as may be seen from the "bodily form" of the descending Spirit. *Much of Luke's understanding of the identity of Jesus is in terms of his possession of the Spirit.* With the Spirit given, Jesus is ready to begin his ministry.

Most modern-day readers of the gospels are surprised to discover that Luke placed Jesus' genealogy at this point in his narrative. Matthew's placement of it at the beginning of his gospel might make more sense, if something so dull as a list of seventy-seven names could be thought to have a purpose. Careful study of this ancestor list, however, reveals that it is a highly theological document. It flows out of the notion that Jesus was beginning his ministry at the age of thirty. This genealogy, therefore, is just as much a statement of Jesus' credentials for that ministry as the story of the descent of the Holy Spirit. To say that he was, "as supposed," the son of Joseph is to give a reminder of Jesus' real parentage and virginal conception. The validity of Jesus' Davidic descent, and thus messianic status, does not depend on biological paternity, since in Jewish law all the children of a man's wife were his legal heirs. The genealogy, however, is not traced back just to David or even to Abraham, the father of Israel. No, the descent is traced to Adam, thus showing that the salvation brought by Jesus was not just for Israel but for all people. John the Baptist has already commented on the irrelevance of Abrahamic ancestry for salvation in 3:8. Jesus' real identity, however, is that he is the Son of God (3:38; cf. 3:22). Jesus is also the Second Adam, in whom the human race is re-created (see Romans 5).

Since John the Baptist disappears after the baptism of Jesus and the story of the baptism is followed immediately by the genealogy of Jesus, a major school of Lukan scholars interprets this section as a literary sealing-off of the ministry of Jesus from that of John so that the two belong to different epochs. So elaborate a thesis is unnecessary when John's subordinate status as forerunner is kept clearly in view. This thesis is supported by an effort to show that the territory in which John operated was different from that of Jesus. That can be done only by assuming that Luke had access to the same information as Matthew and chose not to use it, since Luke gives the same setting for John's ministry that his source Mark does. It is simpler to suppose that Luke was merely following his source than to detect an elaborate effort to restrict the "turf" of Jesus from John's incursion.

By the same token, Luke's injection of the report of John's imprisonment at the end of this section rather than later can be understood as narrative economy, the sort of thing he referred to in his preface as the writing of an "orderly account" (1:3). Luke does, however, refrain from identifying John the Baptist as "Elijah returned from the dead," as Mark and Matthew do. His reason for so doing is apparently that he uses the Elijah motif for both John and Jesus, as he also uses the Samuel motif for both. Thus his failure to treat John as Elijah in this section cannot be taken as evidence that Luke did not understand the relation between John and Jesus as that of messianic herald and Messiah. Such an understanding is quite explicit in 1:76. The effort to put John and Jesus into separate ages therefore fails.

The threefold temptation of Jesus (4:1–13) is a story that Luke shares with Matthew. Mark also tells that Jesus was tempted, but he does not divide the experience into three episodes. This means that Luke's form of the story comes from the sayings source that he shared with Matthew, which scholars call Q for want of a better name. Luke's version of the story is different from Matthew's in several respects, and this has caused some scholars to assume that Luke changed the story for editorial purposes of his own. Each version fits the theology of its editor so well, however, that the originality of Matthew's version cannot be presupposed. One difference between the two is in the order in which the three temptations occur. In Matthew the temptation at the Temple comes second, but in Luke it is third. Luke has many climactic events occur in Jerusalem, and he may have changed the order to let that happen in the temptations, but there is no a priori reason to assume that this was not the sequence of temptations in the sayings source. Further, Luke does not say that Jesus was on a mountain when Satan showed him "the kingdoms of the world." That may have been because mountains are usually places of revelation for Luke. On the other hand, Matthew may have thought that a mountain was necessary for such a vantage point, while Luke recognized more realistically that there is no place on the earth from which all kingdoms may be seen.

This passage is also crucial to the interpretation of Luke that sees him as dividing time into epochs. Since the temptation story ends with Satan's departure from Jesus "until an opportune time," and since Satan is not mentioned again until 22:3, when he "entered into Judas called Iscariot," the claim is made that Satan was inactive between those two appearances. Thus it is argued that the time when Satan was inactive was a time of salvation in which it was possible to foresee what the kingdom of God would be like. Since, however, Jesus continued to encounter opposition from both human and supernatural beings who were under the power of Satan, surely the theory makes too much of the absence of the name Satan from the text. After all, he is mentioned only once again in the gospel after he was supposed to have been reactivated (22:31) and mentioned only twice in all of Acts (5:3; 26:18). It is simpler to suppose that Satan was not very important in Luke's theology.

One is on much surer ground to understand the story of Jesus' threefold temptation in terms of his identity as the Son of God, an identity that had just been affirmed both in the story of the baptism and in the genealogy. Two of the temptations are prefaced with the words "If you are the Son of God. . . ." The issue at stake, then, is what it meant for Jesus to be the Son of God. In part it meant that he was "full of the Holy Spirit" and led by the Spirit (4:1). By resisting the wiles of Satan, Jesus showed that he was indeed the Spirit-filled Son of God. That, at least, is part of the use Luke makes of this story which he inherited from tradition. The story also shows Jesus, the second Adam, reversing Adam's disobedience in his own resistance of temptation, thus picking up on the genealogy that goes back to Adam. With the testimony of John, the descent of the Spirit, the genealogy, and the resistance of temptation, Jesus has been shown by Luke to have all the qualifications necessary for beginning his messianic ministry.

GETTING STARTED

Telling how Jesus began his ministry is a narrative challenge of some complexity. What that ministry was all about must be made clear. The reception it met in various places must not only be reported but also be taken into account. A cast of characters needs to be brought on stage, and the reader needs to be familiar with the kinds of things Jesus said and did. Luke gets this new phase of the story off to a dramatic start with an account of Jesus' preaching in the synagogue at Nazareth, his hometown. This event alone should be enough to refute the thesis that between the temptation of Jesus and that of Judas there was a tranquil time of salvation in the Middle of Time, as advocates of that position call it.

With quick, broad strokes Luke sketches the beginning of Jesus' ministry: "Jesus returned in the power of the Spirit" into Galilee, and his preaching in the synagogues met with instant success. When he returned to his hometown of Nazareth it looked like he would be received there as enthusiastically as he had everywhere else. In this story, Luke gives us more detailed information about what a synagogue service at the time was like than we find elsewhere. Jesus, as the visiting dignitary, was permitted to read the lection from the prophetic scroll and to expound it. The passage selected was Isa. 61:1–2, which has the speaker refer to himself as being *anointed* by the Spirit to proclaim good news to the poor and to bring relief to those who suffer from many kinds of trouble. In his sermon Jesus tells the congregation that the passage is a prophecy concerning himself and that it is coming true before their eyes at that very moment.

The passage had been interpreted messianically for some time. Indeed, the word messiah means "anointed." The great acts of release listed in this passage are signs that the blessings of the messianic age have been made available. Thus it is obvious that Luke understands this sermon in Nazareth programmatically: *It is Jesus' inaugural statement of his mission.* Later in 7:22 the importance of this passage will be made clear. There John the Baptist had sent from prison to learn if Jesus was the coming one, the expected messiah, or not. Jesus' reply was: "Go and tell John what you have seen and heard: the blind receive their sight, the lame walk, the lepers are cleansed, and the deaf hear, the dead are raised up, the poor have good news preached to them." In other words, all the promises of the Isaiah passage are coming true.

The real question, however, is: What went wrong there in Nazareth? At first the entire congregation was quite impressed. Things began to go sour, it seems, when they asked, "Is this not Joseph's son?" Jesus turned on them and said in reply that "no prophet is acceptable in his own country." He then accused them of wanting only to see him perform miracles. His response to that interest of theirs was to tell them of miracles that Elijah and Elisha performed for gentiles instead of Jews. By then they were so angry· that they took him out to throw him over a cliff. What happened? What went wrong? The turning point of the episode occurs when the people ask, "Is this not Joseph's son?" This question shows that they wish to respond to Jesus in terms of his human origin rather than his divine mission. When Jesus detects their motive, he knows that his own people will never take him seriously enough.

This scene is prophetic of all Jesus' ministry and of his eventual rejection by Israel. There is also an implication here of the success that the gentile mission will meet in Acts. This scene, then, is prophetic of both the messiahship of Jesus and its rejection by his own people. It also specifies something of what it means for him to be Messiah: He is a prophet. In addition, something of the character of Luke's understanding of the richness of prophecy comes through in the way that this event is prophetic of all that is to follow. For Luke, events as well as words can be prophetic.

In the next section, Jesus began to carry out the program announced in the synagogue at Nazareth, but in the synagogue at Capernaum, and in the other synagogues in the region, he was accorded the appropriate reception. Throughout this section (4:31–44) Luke follows Mark closely and makes only minute changes. He does, however, postpone the call of the disciples to 5:1–11, permitting himself to contrast with no interruption the receptions that Jesus received in the different synagogues. The postponement also allows him to make more of the call of the Twelve when he does relate it.

In its Markan form, all this material was closely related to the theological emphases of the evangelist. Mark understood Jesus as inaugurating the new age of the kingdom of God by bringing to an end the control over history exercised by the forces of evil until that time. These passages also contained the characteristic Markan theme of the "messianic secret." Most of these themes do not appear to have been as important for Luke as they were for Mark, but Luke uses the material at hand to make his own points.

In the list of healing activities in the Isaiah passage that Luke treats as the program for Jesus' ministry, there is no mention of the expulsion of unclean spirits or demons. Israelite preoccupation with such spirits developed after the Isaiah passage was written. Yet for all three synoptic writers, Jesus' ministry of casting out demons was one of the most important signs of his messianic identity. Incidentally, John makes no mention of such activity. The cure of the demoniac in the synagogue at Capernaum is a main reason for Jesus' success there and for the spread of his fame (4:36–37).

Coming so closely after his rejection in the synagogue in Nazareth, Jesus' success in the synagogue at Capernaum is significant. As suggested earlier, it is prophetic of the success of the gentile mission in Acts after Jesus has been crucified at the instigation of the religious leaders of his own people. The success at

Capernaum is emphasized by the way the people follow him to a lonely place to keep him from leaving them (4:42). In Mark, Luke's source here, it was the disciples who followed him. The people want him to stay, but he has to go on to the other synagogues in Judea (all of Palestine here, not just the southern province). In them the reception of Jesus will be equally enthusiastic. The "good news of the kingdom of God" (4:43) is documented by the cures Jesus performs in fulfillment of the prophecy of Isaiah. By also expelling unclean spirits and curing diseases, Jesus proves that the kingdom is being inaugurated by his proclamation of it. Thus Jesus proclaims the nearness of the kingdom by deed as well as by word.

Although the story of the healing of Peter's mother-in-law came to Luke from Mark, he was probably pleased to have a healing of a woman to balance the healing of the man in the synagogue at Capernaum. He often balances a scene in which a male is central with one in which a female has a prominent role, as when the prophecy of Simeon was followed by that of Anna at the presentation of the infant Jesus in the Temple. *It is characteristic of Luke to show concern for those less favored by society.*

As noted above, Luke did not leave the call of Peter and the sons of Zebedee at the point in the chronological sequence it occupied in his Markan source. Since this group is called some time before the official appointment of the Twelve in Mark, their early appearance was probably a fairly clumsy narrative device to get a cast of characters on stage for the day at Capernaum and the "controversy stories" that follow it. Luke, however, has something different in mind. He must already begin to lay the ground for events that will occur in Acts. For Luke, the main function of the Twelve is not the extension of Jesus' ministry during his lifetime as it is in Mark. It is rather the witness they bear after the resurrection which permits the Spirit-filled community to be formed and spread from Jerusalem to the center of the world, Rome. That witness is prefigured not only by the appearance of characters who will have important roles in that part of the drama, but also by the miraculous catch of fish. As the fishermen caught fish abundantly at this stage of the story, so the fishers of men will convert people in Acts.

The composition of the story about the marvelous catch of fish raises a number of questions for scholars. This setting, which has

Jesus sitting in a fishing boat from which he teaches an audience
standing on the shore, seems to have been borrowed from Mark
4:1. Certainly the punch line about "fishers of men" appears in
Mark 1:17. The story about the catch, however, resembles nothing
else in the Synoptics very closely. The nearest parallel is in the
feeding of the five thousand, in which Jesus is also responsible for a
remarkable increase in the food supply, but the resemblance is not
close. John has the only story that is much like this one, but it
appears as a resurrection story in the appendix to his gospel
(21:4–14). But even here there are as many differences as
similarities. There is much dispute about whether the story belongs
to Jesus' ministry, as in Luke, or with resurrection appearances, as
in John. That need not be a concern of the present study. For
understanding Luke, it is enough to recognize that he used the
story at this point very tellingly to show how the ministry of Jesus
was being extended through the disciples. A typical Lukan touch is
Peter's fear in the presence of the supernatural.

In the series of stories in 5:12—6:11, Luke follows Mark closely,
altering his source only to improve the style or to use terms that
would be more familiar to his Greco-Roman audience. An example
of the former kind of correction occurs when Luke makes it explicit that the tax collector at whose house Jesus ate was the Levi
who had just been converted (5:29; compare Mark 2:15). An example of the latter kind occurs when Luke relates that Jesus cured a
paralytic in a tile-roofed house. Clay tiles were used for roofs
where Luke's readers lived, while adobe roofs of the sort implied
in Mark (2:1–12) were used in Palestine.

When the significance of what happened is made clear to modern
understanding, each of these stories contributes to the reader's
awareness of the significance of Jesus. The healing of the leper, for
instance, was not merely one of Jesus' ordinary healing miracles.
That was not just because the disease can be so horribly deforming.
In fact, what is referred to in the Bible as leprosy was not necessarily Hansen's disease; it could have been something no more serious than psoriasis. All the skin ailments that are lumped together in
the category of leprosy were considered to be ritually defiling. The
sense of supernatural contamination is so strong that leprosy was
said to be cleansed rather than healed. Thus Jesus' ability to cure

this frightening condition was much more impressive than any ordinary miracle-working. In Leviticus 13 and 14 there are rules by which a priest can declare that leprosy had cleared up, but Jesus actually had the power to remove it. The implied argument is that it takes a supernatural person to cure a supernatural disease.

The healing of the paralytic deals with the power of Jesus to forgive sins. Since contemporary belief assumed that only God could forgive sins and that he would not do it until the resurrection, the implied claim about the identity of Jesus is ultimate. Following Mark, Luke refers to Jesus in this story as the "Son of man." This title is the key to Mark's understanding of Jesus, but it should not be assumed that Luke understood it in the same way Mark did. Luke's understanding of the title will have to be gleaned from the way he used it in other places too.

In Jesus' table fellowship with Levi and his friends, Jesus' superiority to all the rules of ritual purity at meals is implied. Since these rules were considered part of the Law that God had imparted to Moses, one is to infer that Jesus has authority superior even to that of Moses. He can repeal what was legislated through Moses. It is even apparent in the discussion about fasting that Jesus' presence on earth permits dispensation from all the ordinary obligations of piety. Jesus was shown to be superior even to the Sabbath, since his disciples were excused from the Sabbath rest and he himself healed on the Sabbath. In what sociologists have referred to as the "disenchanted" modern world, the law against working on the Sabbath, especially when it was extended to such petty matters as plucking grain while walking through a field or even healing the sick, may seem unreal, but it was taken with utmost seriousness in the society in which Jesus lived. When the implications of all these stories are spelled out, therefore, it is clear that Jesus was understood to be more authoritative than all the religious institutions of the Old Testament. He had divine authority. Since, however, Luke is passing on Markan material here with very little alteration, it is not certain that he saw all these implications. He may have been only repeating what had been handed down to him.

After following Mark so closely for a while, Luke suddenly reverses the order of two paragraphs (6:12–19). Mark has Jesus speaking to representatives of the territory of the original twelve tribes of Israel and then drawing from that group those whom he will appoint (Mark 3:7–8). Luke, on the other hand, has Jesus healing the multitude after the appointment of the Twelve. The two evangelists are trying to make the same point about the call of the Twelve. Both see here the symbolic reconstitution of Israel, with each disciple representing one of the twelve tribes. That this is Luke's understanding comes out clearly in 22:30, where Jesus says that the Twelve will sit on thrones and judge the twelve tribes. He reverses the order of Mark's paragraphs in order to prepare a setting for the Sermon on the Plain that is to follow.

As noted above, Luke and Mark emphasize different aspects of the ministry of the Twelve. For Luke their main significance lies after the resurrection, when they will be witnesses to the resurrection. This is demonstrated in the story of the election of Matthias to fill the vacancy left in the Twelve by the apostasy of Judas (Acts 1:15–26). Luke indicates something further of the importance of the Twelve by his report that Jesus prayed all night before appointing them (6:12). Luke also uses the term "apostle" to refer to them, much more often than Mark and Matthew, who use it only once each. The addition of Acts to his gospel gives Luke the opportunity to develop this understanding of the role of the Twelve.

PROPHETIC TEACHING

The Twelve are appointed on the mountain, which in Luke is a place for communication with God. Thus they are taken into the realm of the holy. Then they come down with Jesus to meet the people on the plain of everyday life. Some have been reminded by this of Moses' going up on Mount Sinai to receive the Law and then bringing it back down to Israel. Since Luke writes in the Semitic style of the Greek of the Septuagint whenever he wishes, it is hard at times to know whether he is merely using the language of the Old Testament or whether he wishes the reader to understand the New Testament event in the light of the Old Testament passage from which he borrows phraseology. In Acts 3:22, however, he does make it clear that *he understands Jesus in terms of the "prophet like Moses" described in Deut. 18:19.*

Although the Sermon on the Mount comes at roughly the same place in Matthew as the Sermon on the Plain comes in Luke, and the two start and end with the same materials, there are a number of differences between the two, the most notable of which is length. The sermon in Matthew runs to 107 verses, the sermon in Luke to only 30. Much of the material Matthew puts in his sermon is used by Luke in other places, especially chapters 11–13 and 16. The two are obviously drawing off the same source (Q) but it is impossible to be certain whether one of them has revised the source extensively. In fact, there is no way of knowing that it came to the two of them in nearly identical forms.

Both sermons begin with "beatitudes," statements of the blessedness of certain groups of people. Two words in Greek are translated by the one English word "blessed." The word used here means that the people so described are in a happy or fortunate position; another Greek word is used to say that someone has been blessed by God in the technical sense. Luke's list of beatitudes is less than half as long as Matthew's. He talks only of the good fortune of those who are poor, hungry, weeping, or hated. Matthew's list adds those who are meek, merciful, pure in heart, peacemakers, and slandered. Note that four of Matthew's additions are positive virtues. Even the categories he shares with Luke have been ethicized; he talks of the poor in spirit, and his hungry are those who hunger and thirst for righteousness.

Luke seems to be referring more to those who are actually suffering, the outcast and downtrodden. He also follows his four blessings with four woes, talking about the bad fate in store for those who are rich, well-fed, laughing, and well-spoken-of. The theme is obviously the reversal of fortunes in the kingdom, a prominent theme in the infancy stories. The atmosphere is that of the community of Christian *Anawim*, the "poor" who are the faithful remnant of Israel that has waited for the consolation of Israel and seen it in Jesus the Messiah. Another difference between the beatitudes of Luke and those of Matthew is that Matthew makes abstract, third-person statements ("blessed are *the* poor in spirit") while Luke has the sermon addressed to the disciples in the second person ("blessed are *you* poor").

The beatitudes and woes are statements about judgment, about a radical separation of humanity into two groups. Yet the judgment is not based on socioeconomic conditions alone. Rather, the designations are more theological than they are sociological. The rest of the sermon, as Luke relates it, could be understood as spelling out behaviorally what it means to be poor, hungry, weeping, and hated, that is, what it means to be a disciple, a member of the Christian *Anawim*.

It boils down to a reversal of standards of behavior that is as radical as the reversal of fortunes at the time of judgment is expected to be. Loving enemies, blessing those who hate, and praying for abusers is doing the opposite of what people do to you. Such reversal of treatment is not limited to attitudes or talk but is the standard of action as well: If anyone wants to take anything away from you, give him more than he tries to get. The inner motivation of this is spelled out as the Golden Rule. Its negative form had already appeared in Judaism a number of times: Do not treat others in a way that you would not like to be treated yourself. The Sermon on the Plain/Mount is the first place the more inclusive and demanding positive statement of the rule appears: Give others the sort of treatment you would like to receive. It is only for meeting this radical standard of behavior that one receives any "credit," since those upon whom the woes are pronounced measure up to most lesser standards of conduct. Withholding judgment is included in the ways by which one goes the extra mile and obeys the Golden Rule.

There follows a series of statements on the theme of "by their fruits you will know them," statements to the effect that behavior is consistent with character. One does not ask directions from someone who cannot see. Those whose vision is impaired cannot improve the vision of others. As good trees produce good fruit, good people do good things. Calling Jesus "Lord," therefore, is a commitment to behavior consistent with being one of the Christian *Anawim* who reverse the oppressive treatment of those on whom the woes are pronounced. They thus build their life on solid foundations.

This seems to be the logic that binds the Sermon on the Plain together.

MINISTRY IN ACTION

Luke's literary genius manifests itself most impressively in his construction of individual scenes that evoke an emotional and devotional response on the part of the reader. At the same time, it is easy to detect the large, overarching design of his entire work, the division of his gospel into sections that deal with Jesus' nativity, ministry in Galilee, travel, and stay in Jerusalem, and the division of Acts according to the program of the eighth verse of its first chapter. What is often much more difficult to detect is the interrelatedness of individual stories within these large blocks. Often it appears as if Luke just inserts in no particular order a lot of material he wishes to use. The inner coherence of the material in chapters 7 and 8, at any rate, has not been demonstrated in a convincing way. It merely consists of events that occurred during the Galilean ministry.

Just as Luke and Matthew had to insert the *sayings* material they derived from Q into the Markan chronology at one point or another, so too they had to find room for additional *stories* they wished to incorporate from Q, from their special sources, or from their own creative activity. Having just incorporated a long teaching section from Q in the Sermon on the Plain, Luke turns now to insert six narrative paragraphs not derived from Mark (7:1—8:3).

The first of these is the story of the healing of the centurion's servant. This story is also told by Matthew in a similar position after the sermon (Matt. 8:5–13). It even appears in a different form in John 4:46–54 and is thus one of the few narratives to appear in both the Synoptics and the Fourth Gospel. There are two main differences between Luke's version and Matthew's. The first is that Luke reserves for a later occasion several sayings of Jesus that Matthew attaches to the story. The other is that Luke has the centurion deal with Jesus through intermediaries, never in person. This alteration fits the Lukan habit of not permitting any direct contact between Jesus and gentiles, with the result that *the gentile mission is reserved for the Book of Acts*. The centurion, who is described by his Jewish emissaries as one who "loves our nation, and . . . built us our synagogue," is typical of the God-fearers, the gentiles attached to the synagogue, who appear so often in Acts. In the Synoptics Jesus performs two miracles from afar, this one and the healing of the daughter of the Syrophoenician woman in Mark 7:24–30, and they are both performed on non-Jews. In both cases the faith of the gentiles is said far to exceed that of the Jews. Thus is foreshadowed the gentile mission and the greater acceptability that

Jesus found among those who were not expecting a messiah than among those who were. In the present story, that greater faith is seen in the centurion's understanding of what it means to have authority.

The raising of the widow's son in Nain is a story that appears only in Luke (7:11–17), but Jesus' power to raise the dead is a theme that appears in all the gospels. The raising of Jairus's daughter appears in Mark 5:21–43, Matt. 9:18–26, and Luke 8:40–56, while that of Lazarus is seen in John 11:1–46. The present story is reminiscent of the account of Elijah's raising a widow's son (1 Kings 17:17–24; see 2 Kings 4:18–37 for a similar story, in which Elisha raises the son of a woman whose husband is still alive). The people react to this mighty deed of Jesus by saying, "A great prophet has arisen among us." This is one of the many instances in which Luke interprets Jesus in the tradition of the Old Testament prophets. In this case as in some others, the prophet with whom the parallel is drawn is Elijah, although he could on other occasions draw parallels between John the Baptist and Elijah. Indeed, several things in this story prepare the reader for the question from John the Baptist in the next paragraph.

The other comment of the crowd is that "God has visited his people." The use of the verb "to visit" is reminiscent of the Benedictus that Zechariah said when John was named: "For he has visited and redeemed his people" (Luke 1:68). Visitation is one of Luke's favorite terms for the way God acts for the salvation of his people. It not only occurs in the infancy narratives and during Jesus' ministry, but is used in an especially impressive way when Jesus weeps over Jerusalem "because [it] did not know the time of [its] visitation" (19:44).

In the next story Jesus will respond to John's question about his identity by saying, among other things, that "the dead are raised up" (7:22). This story therefore had to appear first in order to justify that claim. Luke undoubtedly had in mind here not only the resuscitation of corpses during the ministry of Jesus but also the hope of the resurrection from the dead brought to all Christians by the resurrection of Jesus.

John's question from prison, "Are you he who is to come or shall we look for another?" has raised questions since the days of the church fathers. People have wondered if John, who had so much inside information about his cousin Jesus, could have spent his ministry as a forerunner and herald only to wonder at the last if his life's message had been mistaken. As indicated above, the more appropriate question has to do with which passages represent historical reminiscences about John and which have to do with the theological understanding of Luke. John's uncertainty over Jesus' messiahship in this passage is probably closer to history than his explicit identification of Jesus as the Messiah. Luke, however, does not treat the question as if it were inconsistent with anything that had gone before; it is merely John's need for reassurance on a long-held conviction.

The story comes from Q, but Luke adds here—or Matthew leaves out—a number of cures and expulsions of evil spirits so that the messengers will be taking eyewitness accounts of the fruits of Jesus' ministry back to John. It is interesting to set Jesus' answer here parallel to Isa. 61:1–2, the passage he quoted as the programmatic statement of his identity and mission at his inaugural sermon in Nazareth (4:18–19).

Isaiah's Prophecy	*Jesus' Response to John*
The Spirit of the Lord is upon me, because he has anointed me to *preach the good news to the poor*. He has sent me to proclaim release to the captives and *recovering of sight to the blind*, to set at liberty those who are oppressed, to proclaim the acceptable year of the Lord.	Go and tell John what you have seen and heard: the *blind receive their sight*, the lame walk, lepers are cleansed, and the deaf hear, the dead are raised up, the *poor have the good news preached to them*.

To Isa. 61:1–2 should be added 35:5–6: "Then the eyes of the blind shall be opened, and the ears of the deaf unstopped; then shall the lame man leap like a hart, and the tongue of the dumb sing for joy." Thus the meaning of 7:23 is: "Blessed is *John* if he takes no offense in me," that is, if he does not allow any impediment to come between him and the acknowledgment that Jesus is indeed the coming one.

Jesus then goes on to make a definitive statement about his own status in relation to that of John the Baptist. John was a prophet and more: He was the prophesied forerunner of the messiah (Mal. 3:1; note that in 4:5 Malachi identifies that forerunner with Elijah). But John is "less than the least in the kingdom of God." This evaluation does not seal off the ages of John and Jesus from one another, but only distinguishes between the herald and the one he announces. The same is true of Luke 16:16: "The law and the prophets were until John; since then the good news of the kingdom of God is preached."

So interrelated are John and Jesus in Luke's mind that he goes on to say that "all the people and the tax collectors" approved of what Jesus said because they had had the humility and insight to submit to John's baptism. The same, however, could not be said for their religious leaders. "The Pharisees and the lawyers rejected the purpose of God for themselves" in rejecting John's baptism and Jesus' identity. Jesus therefore compared the leaders to spoiled children who did the ancient equivalent of taking their marbles and going home when others were unwilling to play their way. Yet "wisdom is justified by all her children," and the wise had recognized divine truth when it was proclaimed to them and had acted accordingly. Throughout his gospel, *Luke makes a sharp distinction between how the people responded to Jesus and how the hierarchy responded to Jesus.*

The difference in response of the leaders and the people—the poor, the oppressed, and the sinful—is also emphasized in the story of the woman who anoints Jesus, a story which Luke has moved forward from the position in Holy Week that Mark gives it (Mark 14:3–9). The sense of preburial anointing is lost here, but it is replaced by a detailed comparison of the woman's response to Jesus with that of his host, Simon the Pharisee. The explanation for the difference in response is given in the parable of the two creditors, which does not appear in any other gospel. Instead of heeding his pointed remarks about these differences in response, the others present allow themselves to become distracted into shock over Jesus' claim to be able to forgive sins, an issue that had already come up when the paralytic was healed (5:17–26).

This section is followed by a summary statement that tells of Jesus' itinerant ministry among the towns and villages to which he proclaimed "the good news of the kingdom of God." On this tour

Jerusalem, approaches, there are more evidences of Luke's alteration of Mark to suit his own purposes. In Mark there occur at this
point two episodes that Luke has already fitted into his narrative.
Luke had Jesus' rejection at Nazareth take place at the beginning
of his ministry. While that probably makes more sense chronologi-
cally and fits in with Luke's intention to tell the story "in order," it
leaves him without the motivation it gave to the mission of the
Twelve in Mark. By the same token, Luke had sensibly gotten
John the Baptist offstage before the ministry of Jesus began by
reporting his arrest (3:19–20), so he does not have to report John's
imprisonment now when Herod Antipas's curiosity about Jesus
functions as a filler to occupy the time the Twelve are off on their
mission. Luke is thus also able to omit entirely the story of
Salome's dance, which he may have considered unedifying.

After the feeding of the five thousand (9:11–17) Luke will also
omit all the material in Mark 6:45—8:27. This section, which
makes up about one-eighth of Mark, includes Jesus' walking on the
water, the healings at Gennesaret, discussion of what defiles
someone, the healing of the Syrophoenician woman's daughter,
the healing of a deaf-mute, the feeding of the four thousand, the
Pharisees' concern for a sign, Jesus' discourse on leaven, and the
restoration of sight to the man of Bethsaida. The best explanation
for this omission is that Luke considered most of it to be a duplica-
tion of material he had already included. Then too, in Mark most of
these events occur in gentile territory and, as noted above, Luke
carefully restricts Jesus' ministry to Jewish territory. Since Mark
and Matthew did not write their own equivalents of Acts, they had
to include in their gospels any justification they hoped to make for
the gentile mission. Such justification could have been a reason
that Mark and Matthew included this material in their gospels. By
such an omission Luke is able to make a direct connection between
the feeding of the multitude, Peter's confession, and the transfiguration. This narrative compactness, this telling the story "in
order," accounts for much of the popularity Luke has among the
gospels.

Probably the most remarkable thing about Luke's story of the
mission of the Twelve (9:1–10) is that it is followed later by a
mission of the Seventy (some manuscripts say seventy-two) in

10:1–16. It is not said that the seventy-two have "power and authority" for healing as the Twelve are given (9:1), but since they are commanded to heal the sick and preach the kingdom, it is hard to see the functional difference between the ministries of the two groups—or between their ministry and that of Jesus. The Twelve are not sent out two-by-two, as the Seventy are to be (10:1), which may indicate the individual authority of the Twelve as those who will judge the twelve tribes. The overall impression from both these stories is one of the expansion of Jesus' ministry and thus of its success. The tone is very different from that of Mark, in which the mission of the Twelve is a rush to beat an eschatological clock after there has been a lack of response to the ministry of Jesus.

In Mark, Herod is frightened of Jesus, thinking he is John the Baptist come back to life, but in Luke he is only curious about the one who could inspire so many rumors and interpretations. The possible identities Herod had heard assigned to Jesus (Elijah, one of the prophets, John the Baptist) are just those reported as common opinions by the disciples at the time of Peter's confession (9:19). By the same token, Peter's confession that Jesus is "the Christ of God" in 9:20 is ratified by the voice from heaven at the transfiguration only fifteen verses later. The first third of the gospel concludes with resounding testimony to the identity of Jesus.

Nothing is said about the success of the mission of the Twelve, because the report from the Seventy (10:17–20) will suffice for both groups. When the Twelve return from the mission, however, Jesus does not take them to "a lonely place," as he does in Mark. They go instead to Bethsaida. Since Luke's "great omission" of Markan material begins at the end of this story, and since the last of the omitted stories occurs in Bethsaida, this is no more than Luke's way of keeping on the basic path of Markan chronology. He is not consistent in his execution, however. When the Twelve come to urge Jesus to send away the crowd that had followed them, they say they are in "a lonely place" (9:12). Perhaps Luke understood the crowd as having intercepted Jesus along the way to Bethsaida. Jesus' reaction to the urging of the Twelve does not astonish them as much in Luke as it does in Mark.

The story of the feeding of the multitude was one of the most popular narratives in the early church. The Synoptics and John

both tell it, and Mark tells it twice, once with five thousand fed and
once with four thousand. It combines allusions to (a) miraculous
feedings in the Old Testament, such as the manna that was eaten
during the Exodus, (b) the messianic banquet that was a favorite
symbol of God's victory at the end of time, and (c) the Eucharist.
Through Jesus, the Lord "has filled the hungry with good things,"
as claimed in the Magnificat (Luke 1:53). Certainly this miracle is
part of the evidence on which Peter's confession in the following
paragraph is based. The involvement of the disciples in serving is
also symbolic of the way the church in Acts will make available the
salvation Jesus made possible.

The issue of the identity and status of Jesus has never been far
from the surface of Luke up to this point, and in the story of Peter's
confession it is addressed directly. Jesus, having fed the multitude,
prays as he did before the appointment of the Twelve and as he will
do on other solemn occasions. Then he asks the disciples who *the
crowd* thought he was. It should be noted that the miraculously fed
crowd was still standing there and would soon be brought into the
conversation. From now on through the rest of the gospel it will be
important to pay close attention to whom Jesus addresses which
remarks. As noted earlier, the answers the disciples give to Jesus'
question are the suggestions that Herod had heard: Elijah, John the
Baptist, one of the prophets. When Jesus asks who they themselves consider him to be, Peter answers for all and says, "The
Christ of God." Luke has added "of God" to Peter's reply in Mark
and has also considerably altered Mark's understanding of Peter's
reply. In Mark, after Jesus said it would be necessary for the *Son of
man* to suffer and die, Peter tried to talk Jesus out of what he had
just identified as the essence of his vocation, showing that what
Peter meant by "Christ" and what Jesus meant by "Son of man"
were very different roles. In Luke, however, there is no indication
that Peter's understanding is in any way inadequate. *The word
"necessary," which Mark used, not only is picked up by Luke
here, but also is one of his key technical terms.* It means that a
particular event has been a part of God's plan of salvation all along
and that he has revealed it to his people through prophecy. While
Luke does not question the adequacy of Peter's answer, it will
nevertheless not be until after the resurrection that the disciples

realize completely that Old Testament prophecy made it "necessary that the Christ should suffer these things and enter into his glory" (24:26).

The remarks which follow, addressed to "all," say in effect that what is sauce for the Savior is sauce for the saved. Nowhere in the Bible is it made clearer that Christ promises his followers nothing other than to make them like himself in every respect, including his fate. Luke alone specifies that the cross is to be taken up "daily." Sayings to the effect that people will meet with the same reception at the time of judgment that they give to the proclamation of Christ are typical of the preaching of the community that assembled Q. Mark has Jesus say that some of his hearers will see the kingdom of God "coming in power" before they taste death. Luke omits the phrase about coming in power and thus may mean by "seeing the kingdom of God" something like the experience of Stephen in Acts 7:56 rather than the second coming of Jesus (Greek: *parousia*).

The identity of Jesus has not been revealed completely in his being designated the Christ of God by Peter or even in his own statement that the Son of man must suffer, die, and rise. His suffering and humility are but the other side of the coin of his glory which is revealed in the transfiguration and certified by a voice from heaven. The Jesus who is thus revealed is not the preexistent Word discussed in the prologue to John but the glorified Son of man who will come at the end of time.

Luke's source for the transfiguration is Mark, but he adds a number of his own distinctive touches. Just as Jesus prayed before his baptism, the appointment of the Twelve, and the confession by Peter, so he also prays now. Moses and Elijah talk to him about his "departure," his death, which in Greek is referred to as his *exodus* so that the great event of salvation in the new covenant is identified with that of the old. Here too, then, Jesus' death and his glory are seen to be inextricably intertwined. Peter, James, and John, the innermost circle of the Twelve, are with him and caught up in this supernatural event. At first they are excluded and miss the point, with Peter making the inappropriate suggestion about booths that would honor Jesus, Moses, and Elijah equally. Then they are included in the holy as the cloud of the divine presence, seen on *the Exodus*, overshadows them. Their being taken up into the holy is reminiscent of Jesus' taking the Twelve up on the mountain when he appointed them (6:12–13).

The symbolism of the transfiguration story is as compressed as that of a dream. Jesus had been understood all along as if he were a prophet like Moses, as promised in Deuteronomy, and as if he were an Elijah returned, as promised by Malachi. On the Exodus, Moses would enter a booth (tent, tabernacle) on which the divine presence had descended in a cloud, and when Moses talked with God his face would shine so brightly that he had to wear a veil (Exod. 33:9–10; 34:33–35). Yet just as Jesus was superior to John the Baptist, so he was also superior to Moses and Elijah; they could not be permitted to share equal honors with him. Luke, so concerned with offering models for pious emulation, depicts the three disciples as overcome with awe when they went into the cloud and silent when they came out, thus modeling appropriate behavior for an encounter with the holy.

In Mark's account of the trip down the mountain after the transfiguration, the disciples talk with Jesus about Elijah, whom he identifies with John the Baptist. Luke omits this passage, possibly because he applies the Elijah motif sometimes to John and sometimes to Jesus. After descending the mountain, Jesus cures an epileptic boy whom the disciples could not cure, evoking astonishment at the "majesty of God" which, unknown to the people, had just been displayed in a far greater way on the mountain.

The material in 9:43–50 is a drastically shortened version of a section in Mark that fits into a regular Markan pattern. Mark depicts Jesus as making three predictions of his death, and each time that prediction is followed by (a) an inappropriate response by members of the Twelve, (b) some activity by one who is not a follower of Jesus that elicits Jesus' approval, and (c) teaching by Jesus. We have that pattern here where the disciples argue over who is the greatest, and an unknown person casts out demons in the name of Christ. Here, however, Mark's teaching about the disciples' lack of understanding seems to be greatly softened and to mean no more than that they will not understand completely until after the resurrection.

3
Luke's Travel Narrative

LUKE 9:51—19:27

GETTING STARTED

The central section, which now begins, is like a log of Jesus' trip up to Jerusalem, but the trip has no pace or direction. References to movement occur at the rate of about one and a half per chapter, but they provide no more than a loose framework from which stories may be hung and teaching displayed. Spread along here is most of the Q material Luke uses and a good bit of other material about Jesus that does not appear elsewhere in the canonical gospels. This includes such well-loved parables as those of the prodigal son and the good Samaritan. Efforts to order the sequence of material subjectively have fared as poorly as those that have sought a geographical progression. Some scholars have discerned a succession of topics in the travel narrative which corresponds to that in Deuteronomy, but how much more one understands by understanding that is moot. In the presentation to follow, grand schemes will be eschewed in favor of an effort to understand the points made by individual stories.

Even though this so-called travel narrative will soon bog down in a series of unrelated episodes held together loosely by the motif of a journey, the trip starts off decisively enough. "Setting one's face" is a phrase carrying a sense of sternness and determination in the Old Testament. Jesus goes to Jerusalem because "the days drew near for him to be received up" (9:51). The verb translated "received up" is used elsewhere by Luke to refer to the ascension.

Here it obviously includes crucifixion/resurrection/ascension, that is, everything meant by Jesus' *exodus* in the story of the transfiguration.

There is a reminiscence of Deuteronomy in this first story. The messengers Jesus sends ahead to make arrangements remind one of the twelve spies Moses sent out in Deut. 1:24. At the same time, there are allusions to Elijah as well. The words of James and John about fire from heaven are taken from 2 Kings 1:10, where Elijah took the vengeance Jesus refuses to take. By the same token, when someone asked permission to say farewell to his family before following Jesus (9:61), he was asking for a privilege that Elijah gave Elisha (1 Kings 19:20).

Nothing comprehensible is said about why the Samaritans refused to receive Jesus (9:53). This rejection is undoubtedly meant to remind the reader of the rejection at Nazareth at the beginning of the ministry section. The reader of Acts will also remember this rejection when thinking about the conversion of Samaria in chapter 8. The stories about those who wanted to follow Jesus *if* they could find a place to sleep or *after* they had discharged some prior commitment fit very nicely after this event which shows so well how difficult the road to Jerusalem will prove. Only those who put this obligation absolutely first will be able to make the journey.

The account of the mission of the Seventy is written on several levels and is bound to be confusing to any reader who insists on interpreting it literally and on only one level. Luke alone tells of the mission of the Seventy in addition to the mission of the Twelve, even though the instructions to the two groups are identical in some respects. He conceives of the Seventy initially as advance representatives who will prepare Jesus' audiences for him in the towns he will visit. Yet they all go off and return together instead of being sent out at a set time before Jesus is likely to arrive at the towns they are to prepare. Then, too, their instructions sound like they are to conduct independent, self-sufficient preaching campaigns that will not need completion by the preaching of Jesus. The warnings against particular towns in 10:13–15 mention Galilean towns, harking back to the earlier phase of Jesus' ministry, but the mention of these towns is probably more indicative of Luke's desire to use sayings from Q than it is of Luke's geographical ignorance, contrary to the claim of some scholars. A main theme, however, is that this evangelistic activity anticipates what will occur in the gentile mission in Acts. Just as twelve is the number of the tribes of Israel, so seventy is the number of the nations of the world.

The return of the Seventy allows Luke to show that the representatives of Jesus are successful in spreading his victory over the forces of evil, as they will continue to be in the church in Luke's time. This is not because of any merit of their own, but because of the glorious providence of God. "Babes" had received revelations that had been withheld from the "wise and understanding," the disciples had seen what was denied to "prophets and kings." The sense of movement that the mission of the Seventy gives to the travel narrative seems to be the only effort Luke makes to sustain the momentum of the journey motif.

TEACHING ALONG THE WAY

By having the Seventy sent out and return, Luke has probably arrived at a place that he has longed to be. Having taken care of the demands of the story line, he can now relax and settle down to discuss what he wants to: the wonderful teaching of Jesus. He begins with the Summary of the Law (10:27), which he took from Mark's account of Jesus' teaching in Jerusalem during Holy Week. Its appearance at this point makes it the fit beginning of a section of Christian catechesis. Luke's skill as a writer is seen in his unwillingness to leave the Summary as an abstract statement; he has to go on and illustrate its principles in action. The story of the good Samaritan, which occurs only in Luke, shows what it means to love a neighbor. Note that Jesus changes the question from "Whom must I love when I love a neighbor?" to "What should my love look like when I am truly acting as a neighbor?" The quality of love manifested in the behavior of the Samaritan is love for another that is equal to love for the self. Love of God, which has priority over love for a neighbor, is illustrated when Mary sits at Jesus' feet and listens to him rather than being "distracted with much serving" as Martha was.

After the Summary of the Law and its illustration, Luke moves immediately into another favorite aspect of the teaching of Jesus, his teaching on prayer (11:1–13). Like other significant actions of Jesus, his teaching the disciples to pray takes place after he has prayed himself. His prayer at this point may only furnish an occasion for the disciples to ask him to teach them to pray, rather than marking the great solemnity of what is to happen. Luke's form of the prayer is shorter than that in Matthew, having five rather than seven petitions. Those accustomed to the liturgical forms of the prayer often find the Lukan form barely recognizable. Something of its structure in Greek may be seen in this translation:

> Father,
>> May your name be held in reverence,
>> May your kingdom come.
> Give us this day the bread that belongs to it.
> And forgive us our sins,
>> for we also forgive everyone that is indebted to us.
> And do not bring us to the last great trial.
>>>> (Author s trans.)

A little thought will show that when Jesus taught the prayer he meant it to be understood in the context of his teaching that the reign of God was breaking into history through his own proclamation of the fact. Later the extent to which Luke shared that expectation with Jesus will be explored. It is enough at the moment to say that the matter does not seem to have been urgent for him.

Luke's own understanding of the prayer is therefore to be derived more from his references to it in his narrative and the teaching about prayer that he inserts at this point than from the content of the Lord's Prayer as Jesus meant it to be understood. In his comparison of our prayers with the requests that neighbors make at inconvenient times, Jesus' sense of humor shows through. If a fellow human being will give in to one's entreaties just to stop them and get some peace, "how much more will the heavenly Father give the Holy Spirit to those who ask him." *The Holy Spirit is another distinctive Lukan emphasis;* Matthew merely says that the Father will give "good things," a reading much more likely to go back to Jesus.

Luke gives the Beelzebul controversy a setting entirely different from the setting it has in Mark. In Mark it helps establish the theme of the progressive alienation of Jesus; it occurs when Jesus' family seems to think he is emotionally disturbed. In Luke, on the other hand, this story follows Jesus' teaching on prayer, and the charge that Jesus employs demonic power in his mastery over demons grows out of a particular exorcism, the expulsion of a demon that caused the person possessed to be mute. Some members of the crowd offer an explanation for Jesus' miraculous power, namely, that he is in league with the devil. Beelzebu*l* is the Greek spelling of the name of a Philistine god whose name is mockingly changed in 2 Kings 1:2 to Beelzebu*b*, "Lord of the flies." By New Testament times the name no longer refers to the high god of a state cult but has come instead to be one of a number of names by which the prince of demons is called.

In the thought-world in which Jesus taught and Mark wrote, the present age was believed to be an evil age under the domination of the forces of evil. These forces were under the command of the prince of darkness. A glorious "age to come" was expected, in which the control of demons over history would be broken and the rule of God established. This rule, reign, or kingdom of God was to be ushered in, according to some, by God's *anointed* (Hebrew: *mashiach*; transliterated *messiah*). It is not clear how deeply Luke was committed to this doctrine of two ages. He may have simply seen the triumph of Jesus over sickness and unclean spirits to be fulfillment of such prophecies as Isa. 61:1–2.

The member of the crowd who suggests that Jesus uses demonic power to cast out demons adds to the list of possible identities that have been suggested for Jesus. To the list familiar to Herod Antipas and the disciples—Jesus as a revivified Elijah, John the Baptist, or one of the prophets—Luke adds the alternative that Jesus is like the Faust of medieval legend in that he uses diabolical power to accomplish his will. Jesus' refutation is short and commonsensical: If he expelled demons by demonic power Satan would then be fighting against himself, something the prince of demons is far too canny to do. To this, Jesus adds an additional argument providing us with the incidental information that a number of Jesus' contemporaries in Israel were thought to have power to expel unclean spirits. Thus Jesus was unique not in what he did but in how he thought he was able to do it, namely, by the "finger of God." Jesus' argument in relation to the other exorcists is *tu quoque*—"You're another'n," as we said in the rural South when I was a boy. If his power over demons was demonic in origin, so was theirs. But he does not imply the reverse. His own power over demons demonstrates that he is the one promised by the prophets, but theirs shows no such thing about them.

The parable about the "strong man, fully armed" who "guards his own palace" has obviously been altered considerably by Luke, and it is tempting to regard such details as the armor of the strong man as symbolic, although the precise reference is not clear. This parable and Luke's talk in 11:17 about "house falls upon house" (an RSV translation that has been revised in later editions, incorrectly in my opinion) strongly suggest that the desolate condition of Israel after its disastrous revolt against Rome is vivid in Luke's mind. The primary reference, however, is to Jesus as the one who is stronger than Satan and who can therefore wrest the world from his control. There may be a secondary implication that if the people and their leaders had recognized Jesus as the promised prophet, their land would not have been taken away from them. Other passages make it clear that Luke held such a belief, but one cannot be certain whether he is alluding to it here. The ones who do recognize Jesus as the promised prophet are described in verses 27–28 as those who "hear the word of God and keep it." Thus in verse 23 it is they who assist Jesus in gathering, while the ones who do not recognize him are those who oppose him and scatter. Jesus' opponents may have had one demon driven out of them, but they have not prevented him from returning and bringing with him "seven other spirits more evil than himself."

In 11:29–54 Luke has skillfully assembled and woven together a number of sayings of Jesus that had not been related to one another previously. He combines them so that a unified theme runs through them. The issue treated in the preceding section was the failure of people to recognize Jesus. This section tries to offer an explanation for their failure. In the beginning Jesus addresses the crowd to which he had already been speaking but which is now getting larger. Their problem, he says, is that they are looking for a "sign," a miracle to prove beyond a doubt that Jesus is the promised prophet. As we have seen, Luke often uses an implied argument from miracles, but here he recognizes its ultimate inadequacy and has Jesus say that the only sign to be given is the "sign of Jonah." This is to say that the only way he can prove he is a prophet is to preach prophetically. Then he gives two examples of gentiles who have responded to great Israelites in the past: the Queen of the South (Sheba), who came to hear Solomon, and the Ninevites, who repented at the preaching of Jonah. Jesus, however, is greater than either of these worthies of the past, since he is the prophesied Messiah, but his own people are too blind to recognize him.

Next Luke imports two sayings of Jesus having to do with vision, making them refer in this context to the spiritual vision or lack of it in Jesus' audience. In Matthew's version of the saying about an oil lamp put on a lampstand rather than under a basket, the lamp is placed on the stand so it can give light to all in the house, but the reason given in Luke is that "those who enter may see the light." This sounds as if Luke wanted the light to be understood symbolically as Christ, since normally one uses a lamp to see things other than the lamp itself. The idea being put across in the metaphor of the eye is clearer than the language in which it is expressed: the eyes are windows that let in light and thus vision. The word translated "sound" has a basic meaning of singleness; it probably means "clear," in the sense of not being obscured by something like a cataract, although it could refer to the focus of the eyes. Either through a lack of light or through faulty eyesight, those who do not recognize Jesus as the Messiah lack vision.

The scene and the audience change, but the theme remains the same. Jesus goes to eat a meal with a Pharisee. One indication of Luke's middle-class status is the dinner-party setting for so many of the discourses in the travel narrative. Jesus' failure to observe the Pharasaic rules for ritual purity at meals gives him an opportunity to criticize the Pharisees for concentrating on external matters of ceremonial law rather than on more important matters, such as giving alms to the poor. Jesus says that just as people can step on hidden graves without knowing it, so they can pass by the externally righteous Pharisees without being aware of what goes on inside them. Probably the main bad thing that went on inside them was their pride, which prevented their recognizing the Messiah when he came, but there seems also to be a problem of more concern with ceremonial punctiliousness than with the needs of suffering humanity.

One would misjudge Luke completely by taking such settings literally and raising questions about the manners of guests who insult their hosts. Jesus' three woes to the Pharisees and the three others to the students of ceremonial law are given the setting of a dinner party merely to dramatize what would otherwise be an abstract list of condemnations (see Matthew 23). In speaking of lawyers, Jesus gets to the real theme of the passage: Israel's failure to recognize the prophets sent to her. With Luke's prophetic understanding of the status of Jesus, this theme fits right in. Luke also has in mind the situation of the early church, including "apostles" with the prophets who are killed by those to whom they are sent. Jesus says that the blood of all the prophets will be required of the generation to which he was sent, undoubtedly referring to the fall of Jerusalem.

The scene ends with the formation of a plot to force Jesus into saying something that could be used in a trial as evidence against him. Luke has skillfully raised the issue of Jesus' identity and the disastrous consequences of the failure of those to whom he was sent to recognize him.

The material Luke had received about Jesus from tradition was often ill suited to his purposes, yet he was able to draw a verse or two from one source, a few from another, and to blend them with his own special material so that it all fitted together in a new combination which accomplished his purpose and carried his story line. Thus with the Beelzebub controversy in 11:14 he began to distinguish between those who recognized that Jesus was the promised Messiah and those who did not. Luke 11:29–54 was addressed to those who did not recognize him, and now 12:1–53 is addressed to those who did recognize him. In the context of the story these are the disciples, but Luke undoubtedly understood the words as addressed to Christians of his own day as well.

This section begins with the note that "so many thousands of the multitude had gathered together that they trod upon one another" (12:1). Luke has been building up an impression of the increasing popularity of Jesus. While crowds have been referred to all along, the first reference to those accompanying Jesus in the present sequence of events came in 11:14, where the crowd was merely referred to. Then in 11:29 it was noted that "the crowds were increasing." Thus the reference to the "many thousands" in 12:1 is climactic.

Transition is made from the address to those who did not recognize Jesus, most recently the Pharisees and lawyers, by Jesus' telling his disciples to "beware of the leaven of the Pharisees, which is hypocrisy." Hypocrisy can be understood as the concentration on external things which was discussed in the previous section. Such hypocrisy will not work, Jesus says, because the true state of things is certain to be revealed.

When the transition is accomplished and Jesus begins to speak to his disciples about their own condition, it is obvious that Luke has in mind the situation of the church in his own time as much as that of the disciples during Jesus' ministry, because Jesus speaks of the danger of death. Surely the hypocrisy of the Pharisees was not motivated by fear of persecution. After the threat of eternal damnation is contrasted with the lesser danger of death, Jesus goes on to speak of the loving care of God for his children, which extends to knowledge of the number of the hairs on their heads. The decisive factor in determining what one's fate will be after death and who will be the object of such loving concern from the Father is a person's interpretation of Jesus. Does he use demonic power to expel demons or is he the promised Messiah?

By having Jesus say that speaking against the Son of man will be forgiven, but that blasphemy against the Holy Spirit will not be forgiven, Luke probably means to convey that Jews could be forgiven for not recognizing Jesus during his lifetime, but they could not be forgiven for failing to respond to the preaching of the early church about him. Compare Acts 3:17, where Peter tells the crowd that they had acted in ignorance in killing Jesus and that they could repent and still be forgiven.

His own time is foremost in Luke's mind in this discussion of the choice between acknowledging and denying Jesus; this is clear in the instruction to rely on the Holy Spirit when one is brought before "the synagogues and the rulers and authorities" for following Jesus. Along with the fear of death and the love of public recognition (11:43), which could be motivations for not acknowledging Jesus, there is now mention of material prosperity. Jesus refuses to judge between claimants to an inheritance, and he tells the parable of the rich fool, the man who in his comfort neglected the ultimate choice between acknowledging and denying Jesus. A master stroke of Lukan literary art is noticeable when this parable is followed by the long passage about God's care for the birds of the air and the lilies of the field, more often associated with Matthew's Sermon on the Mount than with this Lukan context. Selling one's possessions in order to be able to share with the needy is a way of expressing in action one's decision to affirm rather than to deny Jesus. Such action can be taken only by those who are convinced that it is "your Father's good pleasure to give you the kingdom."

In 12:35–59 a subject which has never been far below the surface emerges into full sight, the time of reckoning. The choice that people make about whether to affirm or deny Jesus will ultimately have its full consequences. In the first statement to the disciples on the subject, the common New Testament metaphor of slaves who wait for the return of their master occurs. By the time of Luke, however, the literal meaning of such language has been all but lost. Luke is so aware that he is talking about the second coming of Jesus that he has the man returning from the marriage feast behave in a manner in which no slave owner would. In modern terms, he takes off his dinner jacket, puts on an apron, and serves a late supper to those who waited up for him. Jesus is the only master who would behave that way.

The reference to the master's coming in the second or third watch of the night indicates that by Luke's time the church had been waiting for Jesus' return for around sixty years. Many scholars think that a crisis of faith had occurred over this delay of the second coming and that a major purpose Luke had in writing was to console the church for this delay. We have very little evidence in the New Testament, however, that the delay occasioned such a crisis of faith.

The metaphor of waiting for the return of the master is succeeded by the equally common metaphor of the time that a burglar breaks into a house. In 12:40 it is made explicit that the future event for which the church needed to be prepared was the coming of the

Son of man. Peter asks if this exhortation is only for the disciples, and Jesus' answer makes it plain that it is addressed primarily to church leaders. In 12:49–50 the coming event is identified as Jesus' approaching death. Thus the story line of Jesus' ministry is picked up again. Yet the division of families over whether to accept Jesus was undoubtedly as acute in Luke's time as it had been during Jesus' ministry.

Jesus then turns to address the crowd about the coming catastrophe. They have sense enough to interpret the weather signs but not enough sense to judge that the events which are occurring all around them were predicted by the prophets. They lack the basic prudence which causes someone with a weak case to settle out of court.

After this long discussion of the coming judgment, Luke has Jesus spell out its implications for Israel. Some of his hearers have reported to him two presumably recent catastrophes, the slaughter of pilgrims en route to Jerusalem from Galilee and the accidental death of some people on whom a tower fell. Neither of these incidents is known to us from other records of the time, but each is quite plausible. One involved Galileans and the other Jerusalem-ites, so the entire territory of Israel is comprehended by the two events. Jesus refutes the commonly held notion of the time that misfortunes and calamities come to people in retribution for sins. His point, however, is not that the people who lost their lives were sinless, but that all in Galilee and Jerusalem were sinful enough to deserve death. Anyone who did not repent would die. God's attitude toward Israel is like that of a vineyard owner who was going to give a barren fig tree one more chance before cutting it down and throwing it into the fire (13:6–9).

What were the Israelites guilty of that they should be so deserving of death? Perhaps the next story is meant to answer that question, since it is set between sections which have very similar meanings. The story recounts a healing miracle, but its real form is that of a controversy story. It has to do with healing on the Sabbath, but it also highlights the kind of issue between Jesus and the Pharisees that was discussed in 11:37–54. The problem is that Jesus' Israelite opponents are so wrapped up in externals that they fail to observe in their very midst the kingdom of God present in such events as the healing of the woman with a spirit of infirmity. The kingdom is growing, though, just as a tiny mustard seed grows into a huge bush, or as yeast makes dough expand.

The question put to Jesus on the way to Jerusalem (13:23) is therefore very apt: Will those who are saved be few? Since the Israelites, bound up in their preoccupation with externals, do not recognize that Jesus is the promised Messiah and that he is ushering in the kingdom, many will indeed seek to enter and will not be able. When they are left out in the cold, they will claim that they have given Jesus more recognition than they actually did, but it will be too late. The patriarchs and prophets will certainly sit down at the messianic banquet with Jesus in the kingdom of God, but the Israelites who heard his preaching and did not accept will be excluded. Instead, their place will be taken by non-Israelites, the gentiles to whom the gospel will be taken in the Book of Acts.

Since an inner coherence that is rare in larger blocks of Lukan material has been detected in the long teaching section (11:14— 13:30), it is worthwhile to review Luke's main points. Jesus (a) has said that the fate of people will depend on their ability to recognize him as the promised prophet, (b) has discussed those who will not and those who will so recognize him, (c) has talked about the end time when the consequences of such recognition or failure to recognize will occur, and (d) has also foretold the gentile mission.

THE JOURNEY CONTINUES

Luke now resumes the journey motif that furnishes the narrative superstructure from which all this teaching material is hung. Pharisees come to Jesus in 13:31 to tell him to leave the country because Herod Antipas wants to kill him. Since Herod was tetrarch of Galilee and Perea, the reader could worry about how little progress Jesus is making in his journey, since after four chapters of traveling he is still in Herod's territory. If it is recognized, however, that the journey functions more as a narrative device than as a chronology, it will be seen that such concerns are irrelevant.

For the same reason, there is no need to ask why Herod, who was merely curious about Jesus in 9:7–9, has now become hostile. Nor is there need to inquire why the Pharisees, against whom Jesus had spoken so strongly in 11:39–44, have suddenly become concerned about his welfare. Since they are urging upon Jesus a course that he does not take—one which, in fact, he considers to be against the divine plan and scriptural prophecy—it is by no means certain that their warning was motivated by friendly feelings.

The real point occurs in Luke's use of two impersonal Greek verbs in verse 33, translated in the RSV as "I must" and "it cannot be." As previously suggested, such verbs in Luke connote activities in which Old Testament prophecy will be fulfilled. Neither Herod nor the Pharisees can arrange for these events to turn out differently. Even the time period, spelled out solemnly as three days but obviously meaning a fixed span of time, has been determined, and it cannot be altered.

Luke uses highly compressed language in 13:31–35. The same word is used in several different senses time and again. This device is brought out very well in a translation of the passage done by David Tiede in *Prophecy and History in Luke–Acts* ([Philadelphia: Fortress Press, 1980], p. 71):

> At that same hour, certain Pharisees approached and said to him, "Depart and *go* from here, for Herod *intends* to kill you." And he said to them, "No, you *go* and say to that fox, 'Behold I am casting out demons and I am *accomplishing* [*apotelein*] cures today, tomorrow, and on the third day I will (be) *complete* [*teleioumai*]. Moreover, *it is necessary* that I *go* my way today, tomorrow, and the day following for *it is not acceptable* that a prophet perish outside of *Jerusalem*.
>
> "*Jerusalem, Jerusalem*, who kills the prophets and stones those dispatched to her. How often I have *intended* to gather your children as a bird takes her brood under her wings, yet you did not so *intend*. Behold, your house is forsaken to you. But I say to you, you shall not see me until [it will come when] you say to me, 'Blessed is the one who comes in the name of the Lord.' " [The italics were added by Tiede.]

From this text one gets a strong impression of the prophet whose death in Jerusalem is prophesied. Incidentally, since none of the writing prophets of the Old Testament was slain in Jerusalem by the leaders and people of Israel, and since Luke produces little biblical evidence that the prophet like Moses was predicted to be killed in the accomplishment of his mission, *the insistence with which he repeats this theme is an impressive indication of how important it was to his theological understanding*. This section anticipates Jesus' entry into Jerusalem when he is greeted by the words "Blessed is the King who comes in the name of the Lord" (19:38) and he again laments over the city (19:41–44). "Your house is forsaken" is another reference to the destruction of the city by the Romans, which Luke understood to be a result of the rejection of Jesus.

Many ancient writers, including Plato, used the narrative device of conversation at a meal as a way of presenting thought. In chapter 14 Luke assembles a number of stories about and sayings of Jesus and organizes them around the setting of a meal that is supposed to have taken place on the journey from Galilee to Jerusalem. Even though Pharisees warned Jesus of danger from Herod in the previous chapter, and even though one is his host in the present sequence, the whole chapter has as its theme the rejection by God of those Israelites (the Pharisees prominent among them) who reject Jesus as the prophesied prophet. As already indicated, a social life characterized by dinner parties is indicative of the middle-class status of Luke and his church. At the same time, Luke is able to present the absolute demands the gospel makes on such people, precisely because he knows what is at stake.

Like the previous banquet, this one proceeds in an atmosphere of hostility between Jesus and his hosts; the Pharisees were "watching him." They entertained the prophet, not to learn from him but to catch him off base and show him up. A person was there with the dropsy, a symptom that the rabbis, who inherited the traditions of the Pharisees, thought was connected with the sins of the flesh. Jesus treated the occasion as a typical instance of the issue of keeping the Sabbath, a regular point of conflict between him and his opponents. While some of the manuscripts make the Pharisees willing to pull "a *son* or an ox" out of the well on the Sabbath, the hyperbole of Jesus' image requires that the correct reading be "an *ass* or an ox." No one will understand this chapter who is literal-minded or who assumes that Jesus was (at least as understood by Luke). Jesus' technique with his opponents is wildly humorous; he indulges in gross exaggeration and caricature in order to make his point. "My God," he seems to be saying, "if you can take pity on—or protect your investment in—a stupid animal on the Sabbath, why can't you do as much for a human being, a child of God?" By making the implicit value system of his opponents explicit, he reveals its shallowness.

One gets the impression that having Jesus as a dinner guest must have been like having Philip Roth. Certainly the wild humor continues in the lesson on hosting banquets. To take this as serious prudential advice would be akin to the way in which Ovid's satirical guide to seduction, *Ars amoratia,* was taken as the textbook on courtly love in the Middle Ages. The last thing that Jesus wanted to tell people was how to keep from getting egg on their faces. The literal-minded could also enjoy turning Jesus' advice about whom to invite to dinner parties into a new law. Implicit value systems, however, constitute what is at stake.

One of the pious hosts tries to salvage the evening for edifying discussion by making a sententious remark about the messianic banquet (14:15). Jesus responded by telling a story about a man who threw a huge dinner party. According to the custom of the time, he sent around a slave to inform the previously invited guests that the meal was ready. The guests, however, made trivial excuses—though possibly for coming late rather than for missing the whole event. The host was so angered that he told his slave to fill up all the places at the meal with bums from the park benches so that when those originally invited got around to showing up they could not find a seat. "The poor and maimed and blind and lame" who were thus rounded up to attend the party were exactly the guests whom Jesus had said (v. 13) should have been invited in the first place.

The servant was sent first to the "streets and lanes of the city" and then, when he did not find enough potential guests there, to the "highways and hedges." This is undoubtedly a reference to the gentile mission, an implication that the pious Israelites who had turned down Jesus' invitation to the kingdom of God would be replaced first by the outcasts of Israel and then by foreigners. The radicalness of the invitation to the kingdom is indicated when it is made clear that one's preference for it should make one's loyalty to even the highest human obligations look like hatred in comparison. Accepting the invitation would be like accepting an invitation to be crucified. It was the sort of thing that prudent middle-class people who made up Jesus'—and Luke's—audience would weigh as carefully as a building project or a war. Yet the losses on one side were so much worse than those on the other side that no sane person would hesitate a second. The reaction of his hearers, however, had indicated that they were not sane; anyone with such an inverted value system could not be. Thus they were like salt that had gone bland and were no longer fit even to be thrown on the manure pile. While these last words were not addressed to his host and fellow guests at the dinner party but to the great multitudes that accompanied him along his journey, Jesus obviously was intended by Luke to be making a judgment on the attitudes expressed or implied at the banquet.

Chapter 15 consists of three parables, the lost sheep, the lost coin, and the prodigal son, all of which have the same point. The first of these appears also in Matthew and probably goes back to Jesus. While such an origin is less certain for the other two, their teaching can be assumed to be consistent with his. The situation of this teaching in the ministry of Jesus is clear: He found it necessary to justify to his opponents his concern for the *Am ha-aretz,* the people of the land, who did not observe the Law with the punctiliousness the Pharisees thought necessary. That is similar to the setting in which Luke places these stories: He has Pharisees and scribes murmur against Jesus because he received and ate with people who did not keep the dietary laws. Because of this setting, and because the lost coin, sheep, or son was of the same kind as those that were not lost, it is plain that Luke does not understand this teaching as a justification for the gentile mission. Instead, he probably means it to refer to "the poor and maimed and blind and lame," twice referred to in the previous chapter. Thus the reference is probably to the Christian *Anawim,* to whom allusion has been made frequently, especially in the discussion of the infancy narratives. As late as the end of the first century, Christians were still having to defend the presence in their midst not only of gentiles but also of Jews who did not come from the social classes that were able to live in ritual purity.

These three parables offer excellent examples of the way Jesus argued his case with his opponents. He would tell a story that he and they could agree offered a valid analogy to the point at issue. He got such agreement by offering an initial concession to their point of view, seen in the present case in the admission that the sheep, coin, or son was lost—and that the son, at any rate, deserved to be. This attitude—"they brought it on themselves"—was one appropriate way of regarding the outcasts of society. When Jesus suggests parabolically that another way of looking at the situation—God's way—is to greet the repentance of such persons with the joy with which one greets the recovery of what had been lost, his opponents are forced to consider that new perspective. Note that the only time one sheep is more valuable than ninety-nine or one day's wages worth nine is at the moment of recovering what had been thought to be irretrievably lost. Luke does not tell us how the father felt about his spoiled son six weeks after he came home. It is at the moment of recovery that the joy is overwhelming, a point which gets repeated in the father's explanation to the elder son of the "barbecue."

The parable of the dishonest agent (16:1–9) has all the delightful amorality of Saki's story about the "horribly good little girl" who upon being allowed to walk in the king's forest was discovered by a wolf and gobbled up when her three medals for good behavior clinked against each other. The literal-minded have been trying to clean it up ever since it first appeared, but it is to be taken in the spirit of the outrageousness of Jesus' table talk in chapter 14. The steward had only one virtue: He had enough sense to know what was going on, what game was being played. When he saw that he was going to lose the job he had, he set about making certain he had a place to jump. He acted with the prudence of the man who finds out whether he has enough capital before he launches on a business project or if he has the troops before he goes to war (14:28–32). Thus he is unlike the first guests invited to the banquet, who did not know they had only one chance (14:15–24).

Since this parable was addressed to the disciples, it could be thought to be a challenge to Christians to be watchful while waiting for Jesus' second coming. It was overhead by the Pharisees, however, and their response gave Luke an opportunity to accuse them of being lovers of money. In a way, the unjust steward was also a lover of money, but he knew how to spend it in face of the challenge of an emergency. As noted before, possessions were for Luke a symbol of people's attachment to their comfort, an attachment that rendered them incapable of responding to the crisis of the Christian message appropriately. That assumption seems to lie behind the statement of Father Abraham that the five brothers of the rich man in Hades would not respond "even if someone would rise from the dead" (v. 31). The leaders of Israel were so much at ease in Zion that they could not see that the testimony of "Moses and the prophets" to Jesus was being fulfilled before their eyes. They scoffed when Jesus tried to warn them of the crisis his preaching brought about.

Chapter 17 begins with four apparently unrelated sayings taken from Q. They deal with the danger of enticing others into sin, the frequency with which Christians should be willing to forgive one another, the power of faith, and the impossibility of putting God in one's debt. The story that follows in verses 11–19 raises a number of questions for the careful reader, beginning with the geographical notation of the opening sentence: "On the way to Jerusalem he was passing along between Samaria and Galilee." This sounds as if one of these areas was to the west of the other, so that Jesus was going southward along the border between them. Since, however, Samaria is south of Galilee, and it is further surprising that Jesus should still be so near the territory in which he began his journey eight chapters earlier, it seems unlikely that Luke was familiar with the geography of Palestine. The fact that the leper who returned to give thanks was a Samaritan probably suggested to him that the story should be given a setting near Samaria.

Most of the questions the story raises, and most of the efforts to find rational answers to them, ignore Luke's propensity to concentrate more on telling an edifying and dramatic story than on making all the details consistent. There are two main points of interest here, the rarity of gratitude and the superiority of the Samaritan. The story is told so as to demonstrate the rarity of gratitude. Thus it is different enough from other healing miracle stories to have caused some scholars to wonder if this is a parable turned into a story about Jesus, an explanation that seems overly mechanical in its view of tradition. The favorable view of the Samaritan does not indicate a "Samaritan source," but requires the low expectation of Samaritans held by Jerusalemites to be dramatically effective. The ending implies that the Samaritan's gratitude gained him some blessing beyond the cleansing the other nine lepers received, but the nature of it is not specified.

In 17:20 Jesus is asked by the Pharisees when the kingdom of God will come, and he tells them it is "in the midst" of them, whatever that means. A favored translation through the years has been, "the kingdom of God is within you," but Jesus would hardly have said that to the Pharisees. "In your midst" could mean that the eschatological age had already been inaugurated, although it does not seem to mean that here. Perhaps in the ministry of Jesus one had a foretaste of the kingdom. Perhaps it meant that the kingdom was "upon" them, or that it was "just around the corner," as the expression "the kingdom of God is at hand" seems to mean. The very least one can say is that the expression is not self-explanatory.

When Jesus turns and addresses the disciples, he does not clear up the situation. To begin with, he talks about the Son of man rather than the kingdom of God, and he proceeds to talk about "one" of his "days." This could mean that there would be a number of such occasions, but it more likely refers to the second coming of Jesus, which could be expressed as the *day* or *days* of the Son of man. It is said that the disciples will wish to see it and will not do so. This is as close as Luke comes to saying that the church in his time was disappointed over the delay of the second coming. At any rate, Jesus is very clear that the time of the days of the Son of man is not very predictable, that there will be no series of signs to enable the observer to keep track of the apocalyptic countdown. It will come as suddenly as lightning lights up the sky when people are engaged in their ordinary occupations. Thus one should always be ready. But when it comes, its presence will be no more mistakable than that of an overripe carcass in the vicinity.

Chapter 18 opens with the parable of the unjust judge who decided to vindicate a poor widow rather than to be annoyed by her constant requests, a point very similar to that of the parable of the neighbor at midnight (11:5–9). The humor, though, is reminiscent of that of the corrupt steward (16:1–9). Here, however, the teaching on prayer is given an eschatological application: God is to vindicate his elect.

Next comes the parable of the Pharisee and the customs collector. Contemporary Christians have become so accustomed to identifying with the penitent "publican," as the King James translation calls him, and to feeling superior to the self-righteous Pharisee that it is easy for them to ignore how radical and outrageous this parable is to middle-class values. The religious duties the Pharisee is grateful for being allowed to perform reflect his party's efforts to "build a fence around the Law," to do what the Torah requires and a little bit more to make certain all of it is obeyed. Thus he fasts and tithes much more than is required. The point of the parable is missed if the sincerity of his gratitude is doubted. He found great joy in the performance of his religious duty, and he thanks God that he was born into a station of life that made it possible for him to perform it. He would have taken no pleasure in a dishonest profession, or even one that would have interfered with his religious duties. His life in praise of God is one in which he takes great pleasure.

The customs collector, on the other hand, knows that his profession is extortionate by its very nature and probably sacrilegious, yet he makes no effort to reform. To do so would deprive him of a business in which he has a large investment. He makes none of the offers of restitution and amendment that Zacchaeus will make in 19:8. Instead, he kneels and beats his breast in despair, knowing that he has no call on God's mercy. Yet because of this he was the one God regarded as righteous, no matter who may have been so regarded by themselves or others. Such is the paradox and scandal of this radical parable. Brilliantly, Luke follows this parable with the account of Jesus' encounter with the rich ruler, which has a different setting in Mark and Matthew. Thus he is able to ram home again the point that the only issue at stake is accepting or rejecting Jesus and the conditions of his call. No other virtue is to be weighed. As Jesus tells the disciples, no one who has forsaken anything for the kingdom "will not receive manifold more in this time, and in the age to come eternal life" (18:30).

For most of the last nine chapters, Luke has been using the narrative motif of a journey from Galilee to Jerusalem as a frame on which to hang most of his teaching material, derived mainly from Q. From now on he will be drawing on Mark as his main source, and there will be relatively more action and less talk. The

Twelve are reminded in 18:31 of the destination (Jerusalem) and purpose (fulfillment of prophecy) of their journey. Unlike Mark, who has made the progressive alienation of Jesus a major theological theme of his narration, and who therefore made much of the secret of Jesus' messiahship, Luke has been preoccupied with Jesus' death as a key element in God's plan of salvation that was foretold in the Old Testament. Thus the disciples are as lacking in understanding here as they are in Mark, but the reason is ignorance rather than hardness of heart. The extent of the misunderstanding is nonetheless so great that it takes three synonymous phrases to express it: "They understood none of these things; this saying was hid from them, and they did not grasp what was said" (v. 34). As will be seen in the Book of Acts, such misunderstanding is not final; the resurrection will make available all necessary explanations. The ignorance is not necessarily culpable yet, but it will be for those who refuse to heed the postresurrection preaching of the apostles.

It often happens in Luke, though not so often as in John, that a teaching of Jesus is closely related to a miracle story or other narrative in which the teaching is illustrated symbolically. That happens now with the story of the healing of the blind man, called Bartimaeus in Mark but unnamed in Luke. The blind man addresses Jesus as "Son of David," anticipating the entry into Jerusalem that will soon follow. The blind man is "saved" by his faith, which thus stands in contrast to the disciples' lack of understanding. The sight he has is therefore spiritual as well as physical. Thus he follows Jesus, "glorifying God." The people, who have also "seen," also praise God.

This account of a blind man's recovery of sight is followed by that of a tax collector, indeed a "chief" tax collector, who "sees" Jesus and accepts the "salvation" he brings. During the time of Jesus, Israel was under a double set of taxes, a civil one to Rome and a religious one to the Temple. This dual burden of taxation combined with the overpopulation of the country and its relatively low productivity meant that times were hard. Roman officials collected tribute and property taxes themselves, but they farmed out the right to collect tolls for the transportation of goods, including slaves, over land or sea. Since the collectors engaged in competitive bidding to secure these toll-collecting franchises, they obviously expected to make a profit through extortion. The Jews who purchased these franchises were despised as ones who collaborated with the enemy that had conquered their country and usurped the kingship of God over Israel. Furthermore, the social contact that such toll collectors had with the gentile Romans rendered them incapable of observing the laws of dietary purity. No wonder these officials were so easily linked with sinners! To their number belong Zacchaeus and the collector in 18:9ff.

Zacchaeus, however, represents the sort of social outcast who was receptive to the good news that Jesus brings, a familiar figure in Luke. Spiritually, he was much more discerning than the Pharisees and other religious leaders who looked down on him. He was even more discerning than the Twelve, who did not understand Jesus' prediction of his death (18:34). He sees the consequence of his acceptance of Jesus without having to have it pointed out to him: he volunteers half his fortune to the poor and to repay quadruply anyone he has defrauded. Thus Luke shows again the connection between one's attitude toward Jesus and one's attitude toward possessions. Jesus' response to Zacchaeus was that salvation had come to his house and that it was precisely such lost children of Abraham whom he had come to save.

Matthew's form of the parable of the talents/minas is far more familiar to most people than Luke's, so special effort must be made not to transfer to one's interpretation of Luke anything remembered from Matthew. The sum of money involved in the two accounts differs considerably: the talents of Matthew are worth sixty of the minas of Luke. It is always misleading, however, to try to set exact contemporary dollar equivalents to biblical coinage. The important thing here is that a mina is enough to set someone up in business.

The setting of the story of Luke concerns speculation about the time of the appearance of the kingdom of God: Would it be ushered in when Jesus arrived at Jerusalem? Jesus' reply is the parable, which in Luke is either a combination of the parable of the "pounds" with one about a nobleman who went away to inherit a kingdom, or an embellishment of the pound parable with details that Luke intends to interpret symbolically. Since Jesus is obviously the nobleman who went away, and Israel the people who did not want him to rule over them, the parable is a way of saying that the kingdom would not come until Jesus' second coming. Before that happens Jesus will be rejected by the leaders of Israel and some of the people, and the leaders of the early church will have an opportunity to test their stewardship in the gentile mission. In interpreting the story this way, Luke does not necessarily postpone the predicted time of Jesus' return much later than the time of writing. The details of the story, incidentally, seem to be patterned on events that occurred after the death of Herod the Great in 4 B.C. His son Archelaus went to Rome to have his father's kingdom transferred to him, but when the Jews sent an embassy saying they did not want him as king, he was given only a part of his father's territory, Judea and Samaria. Even that was taken away from him ten years later, and the territory was placed under a Roman procurator; Pontius Pilate succeeded to the job twenty years later.

4

Climax in Jerusalem

LUKE 19:28—24:53

THE MESSIAH COMES TO THE TEMPLE

Now come the events to which everything that has gone before has pointed: Jesus' death, resurrection, and ascension. At this point in the story one must be aware that Luke's understanding of these events is very different from that of Mark and Paul. Luke does not understand the crucifixion in terms of vicarious atonement, or of sacrificial death on behalf of others. In many ways, Luke has more of a theology of glory than a theology of the cross. His interpretation of the death of Jesus does not go much beyond the recognition that it was the medium of salvation which was planned by God from the beginning and which the Holy Spirit caused to be promised by the prophets. Why God should have willed to redeem humanity that way, or what there is redemptive about the death on the cross, appear not to be questions that occurred to Luke. He was so preoccupied with the triumphant miracle of prophecy fulfilled that nothing else seemed to matter. It should also be remembered that the crucifixion and resurrection did not fulfill all prophecy. All the events recorded in Acts were still to come, as were also the destruction of Jerusalem and the days of the Son of man, the second coming of Jesus to judge the world.

Luke's story of the entry into Jerusalem follows Mark's rather closely, although it omits both Mark's efforts to fit the events of Jesus' ministry in Jerusalem into a Holy Week and his enacted parable of the cursing of the fig tree that is sandwiched between the entry into the city and the cleansing of the city. Both because of the lack of a Holy Week chronology and because Luke does not mention the waving of branches, it is inappropriate to speak of "Palm Sunday" in Luke. Much of Luke's motive for curtailing Mark's account seems to be narrative economy and flow.

Luke specifies that the multitude's song of praise began as Jesus and his party started the descent from the Mount of Olives. Mark's designation of Jesus as the heir of David is omitted here, having been supplied just before in the story of the healing of the blind man (18:38–39). Instead, Luke has the disciples shout, "Peace in heaven and glory in the highest." This greeting recalls the song of the angels to the shepherds in 2:14, but peace has changed its habitation; for the time being, it is in heaven rather than on earth. The Pharisees make what is virtually their last appearance in the gospel when they call Jesus "teacher" and ask him to quiet his disciples. Jesus replies that if the disciples were silent the very rocks would cry out. To the end, therefore, the Pharisees have remained blind to the evidence of Jesus' identity.

In a manner reminiscent of 13:31–35, Jesus weeps over the city and visualizes in detail the Roman siege that will be one of the consequences of the city's rejection of him. Luke's four-stage eschatology, involving (1) crucifixion and resurrection, (2) gift of the Spirit and gentile mission, (3) destruction of Jerusalem, and (4) the second coming, does not constitute an apocalyptic countdown, because the interval between stages was not of a set duration. When Luke was writing, everything had taken place except the second coming, and so he thought the church should be in a constant state of preparedness.

Luke's account of the cleansing of the Temple is much shorter than Mark's or Matthew's. After that, Jesus teaches in the Temple daily. Since the other Synoptics say the same thing, it is unclear whether Luke thinks Jesus cleansed the Temple in order to replace it in his own person and thus become himself the center of Israel, or whether Luke's motivation in shortening the narrative was merely stylistic.

The picture of Jesus teaching in the Temple is even less detailed in Luke than it is in Mark. Nothing interrupts the sequence of the

religious leaders' efforts to collect evidence against Jesus so they
will be able to bring charges against him before the Roman gover-
nor. In Jerusalem these Temple officials replace the Pharisees as
Jesus' opponents. At first they ask him about the authority by
which he made his triumphal entry and cleansed the Temple. To
show they are not taking seriously the messianic authority implied
in those actions, Jesus asks them about the authority of John the
Baptist, about which there should have been no question. Instead
of responding to the question theologically, however, they respond
to it politically, thus demonstrating that serious discussion with
them was impossible. Jesus' reaction is to launch a counteroffen-
sive, using a parable to compare the leaders to tenants who killed
the landlord's beloved son in an effort to expropriate his land for
themselves. Jesus concludes by saying that the landlord will come
and destroy the tenants and give the vineyard to someone else. His
point is not lost on the religious establishment, who know that he
poses an ultimate threat to them and the religious institutions they
lead. Their desire to crush him only increases.

The next effort was to catch Jesus on the horns of a dilemma
much as he caught them in his question about the authority of John
the Baptist. They sent spies disguised as sincere seekers-after-
truth to ask him about paying tribute to the Romans. They assumed
that they had him either way: If he said they should pay, he would
lose his popularity with the people, but if he said they should not,
he could be charged with inciting rebellion. Instead he demonstrated their own involvement in the Roman occupation by having
them produce a Roman coin. Besides, Caesar's image on the coin
showed that it belonged to him and that it was only fair he should
have it.

The entire religious establishment included not only Pharisees,
who believed in resurrection, but also Sadducees, the conservative
high-priestly party, who did not believe in resurrection because it
is not clearly taught in the Old Testament books they accepted as
inspired. They asked Jesus a trick question about resurrection
which involved the Old Testament regulation according to which
the nearest male relative of a man who died without children
should marry the widow and produce heirs for the deceased (Deut.
5:5–10). Jesus showed the foolishness of their objection to the

resurrection by pointing out that there is no need for marriage in the afterlife because no one dies again and thus there is no need to replenish the population by propagation.

After that, Jesus took the initiative and began to ask them questions. He began with the issue of Davidic messiahship. They expected a messiah who would come as a warrior to drive out the Romans as David had expelled the Philistines. Jesus' refutation involved the methods of biblical interpretation in use at the time. He assumed that the Holy Spirit inspired all scripture, that the Psalms were written by David, and that Psalm 110 is about the messiah. That being the case, David would be calling the messiah Lord, thus recognizing his superiority. Since the messiah could not derive his authority from an inferior, the messiah could not owe his status to Davidic descent.

This series of controversies that occurred while Jesus was teaching in the Temple was brought to an end by a personal attack on the scribes in which Jesus repeated the by now familiar accusation that they were avaricious. They enjoyed the attire, the respectful greeting, and the places of honor to which their positions entitled them, but even though they prayed long prayers, they devoured widows' houses. Jesus did not have to wait long for confirmation of his charge. He and his followers stood in the court of the Temple near one of the contribution boxes and watched those who made offerings. According to Jesus, a widow who offered some of the smallest coins was more generous than anyone else because she gave what she needed to live on while others only gave some of their discretionary income. The religious leaders then gave less than a poor person of the sort from whom they had extorted their wealth. Thus the entire religious system was condemned and its arguments shown to be specious.

Mark reports only two long speeches by Jesus, the one about parables in chapter 4 and a revelation (Greek: *apocalypsis*, from which we get "apocalypse") of the end time that lies ahead. Luke 21:5–38 is based on Mark 13, where the "Little Apocalypse" appears and the alterations of his sources that Luke made are very instructive both about the time in which Luke wrote and about his purpose in writing. The leading contemporary school of Lukan interpretation uses this chapter to argue that Luke wrote to console the church about the delay of the second coming. It is certainly true that Luke interprets this speech to refer to events that have transpired between the ministry of Jerusalem and the writing of the gospel. That does not mean, however, that Luke thought the second coming had been postponed to the indefinite future and that the church should settle down to the long haul of history. As will become apparent, Luke thought the end was near when he was writing.

The speech gets off to a simple start. While Jesus was teaching in the Temple, members of his audience made remarks—like tourists do—about the building. Jesus responded by saying the whole thing would be torn down. His hearers acted as straight men, supplying him with the question that was the cue for his discourse: "When will this be, and what will be the sign when this is about to take place?" In effect their question was, "Tell us your eschatology, your theory about the end of the world." Note that in Luke the question and its answer are public utterances, not something private between Jesus and the disciples, as in Mark 13:3.

Jesus predicts that there will be many false alarms about the end of time and the time of his second coming. The occasion of such expectations will apparently be "wars and tumults." The word translated as "tumults" in the RSV, however, should have been rendered "insurrections." It becomes apparent in the course of the speech that Luke understands the occasion of all this false messianic expectation to have been the effort of Israel to throw off the yoke of Roman occupation in A.D. 66–70. Throughout this whole passage there is a double perspective on time. In some places the temporal perspective is clearly historical; it is the perspective of Jesus in Jerusalem before his death. At other times, the perspective is that of Luke and his church some fifty to sixty years later, well after the Jewish-Roman War.

The war is not the only thing that has intervened between the time of Jesus and the time of Luke. All the events involved in the spread of the church from Jerusalem to Rome which make up the contents of the Book of Acts also occurred in the interim. These are the events referred to in verses 12–19. Christians would be persecuted; tried before synagogues, kings, and governors; thrown into prison; betrayed by friends and relatives; and hated by all. Verse 18 seems to be a contradiction to everything that has immediately preceded it in its promise that not a hair of the Christian's head would perish. The resolution of this apparent inconsistency occurs in the following verse, where it is clear that eternal salvation rather than temporal safety is what is promised.

The theme of the destruction of Jerusalem in A.D. 70 recurs in verses 20–24. Apparently, Christians are warned to flee from the city during this time, since the fate of the city and its Temple has nothing to do with the new religious dispensation inaugurated by Jesus. Luke may have been drawing on a historical reminiscence here, because the early church historian Eusebius tells us, "The members of the Jerusalem church, by means of an oracle given by revelation to acceptable persons there, were ordered to leave the city before the war began and settle in a town in Perea called Pella" (*Ecclesiastical History* 3.5). Luke describes this time of crushed revolt as "days of vengeance, to fulfill all that is written," reflecting his belief that the destruction of Jerusalem and the Temple was the prophesied result of Israel's refusal to recognize that Jesus was the promised prophet and Messiah. The section ends with a prophecy of the captivity of Jerusalem until "the times of the Gentiles are fulfilled."

One of the most cryptic statements in Luke is 21:32: "This generation will not pass away till all has taken place." The saying comes through Mark and is also quoted by Matthew, but because the three synoptic evangelists have different understandings of the events connected with the end, what the statement means in one is not necessarily what it means in another. The main question in regard to Luke is, Which generation is *this* generation, the generation of Jesus or that of Luke? Perhaps the answer makes no difference. There were probably Christians who had heard Jesus preach who were still alive in Luke's time. The main point is that *Luke expects the second coming to occur very soon after the time of writing*. He has Jesus offer a parable to the effect that just as the appearance of leaves on the trees indicates the approach of summer, so a series of natural calamities is about to take place that will indicate the second coming is near. For Luke three terms appear to be synonymous: the second coming (Greek: *parousia*), the coming of the kingdom of God (21:31), and redemption (21:28).

The real audience Luke has in mind for the close of this apocalyptic discourse is the church in his own time. It is members of the church who are in danger of being distracted by the pleasures and business of life so that they cease to wait in joyful expectation for the return of the Son of man.

The teaching of Jesus in the Temple precincts that has been going on since the cleansing of the Temple is now brought to an end with a few explanatory remarks about the conditions under which it took place. By reserving this setting until now, Luke has been able to keep Jesus in the Temple through this whole section.

THE PROLEPTIC BANQUET

Luke sets the *exodus* (Greek of 9:31) in the context of the Passover by which *the Exodus* of Israel was initiated. While so doing he is still able to shorten the Markan story of the preparation for the Last Supper, in part because he has not followed Mark's scheme of a Holy Week. Furthermore, by having told the story of Jesus' anointing by a sinful woman (7:36–50), he is able to speed up the story. This allows him to move directly from the conspiracy among the chief priests and scribes to their contract with Judas for betraying Jesus to them at a time the crowd was not around. Luke attributes Judas's betrayal to Satan, who had entered him. The early church had to suffer many taunts, because its Lord for whom it claimed omniscience had apparently not been able to recognize this capacity for betrayal in one of his closest followers. Satan has not been mentioned since the temptation of Jesus, after which it was said that "the devil departed from him until an opportune time" (4:13). Whether now was the opportune time, or whether Luke simply did not often refer to satanic activity, this lack of reference does not furnish an adequate basis for the elaborate theory of some scholars that the time between these two appearances of Satan was "the time of salvation" in which the disciples had a foretaste of the kingdom.

The arrangements for the Passover meal were made by Jesus and involved miraculous foreknowledge rather than prearrangement. One change that Luke makes in the Markan order of events at the Last Supper is to have the institution of the Eucharist occur before

Jesus' prediction that he would be betrayed by one of his disciples. The effect of this order is to show that infidelity is possible even within the eucharistic community, the church, a theme that fits with Luke's constant exhortations to watch and not be caught off guard by the returning Lord. The Passover is treated as refreshment for Jesus before his suffering. In a passage that has no parallel in Mark or Matthew, Luke has Jesus say that he will not eat it again until it is fulfilled or perfected in the kingdom of God, by which he refers to the messianic banquet at the time of his second coming. Some confusion is caused by the reference to two cups—in the best manuscripts of Luke. In the other manuscripts the usual order of bread and wine is reversed. Since more than one cup of wine was consumed at Passover meals, it seems likely that the longer, "two cup," reading was the original one.

When Jesus said that he would be betrayed, the disciples moved from a discussion of which one would be guilty to an argument over which was the greatest. Most of what Jesus says in response is borrowed from his reaction in Mark 10 to the request of James and John to sit at his right and left hands when he came into his kingdom. But Luke ends the discussion with a promise that the Twelve will eat and drink at Jesus' table in the kingdom and sit on twelve thrones judging the tribes of Israel. The time of the kingdom would come after the second coming, but the activity of the Twelve in the beginning of Acts constitutes in Luke's view itself an act of judgment on the twelve tribes or else represents an anticipation of coming judgment on them. At any rate, the Twelve were intimately involved in the renewal of Israel that was to take place through Jesus. This is made clear in Luke's softer prediction of Peter's denial. Jesus tells Peter that he has prayed for him, so that when he has "turned again" he will strengthen his brothers, undoubtedly in his leadership role in the Jerusalem church.

Meanwhile, the disciples had to prepare for the ordeal ahead. When Jesus had sent them out preaching, they had needed no provision for the way, but in the evil times ahead they would need provisions for the journey and a sword for protection. While these verses have been interpreted in many ways, it appears likely that the time of the crucifixion is seen as the prophesied time of the rejection of the messiah. As noted before, Luke's basic interpretation of the death of Christ focuses more on this element of the fulfillment of prophecy than it does on the element of vicarious suffering so prominent in Mark and Paul. There lies ahead an ordeal unlike any that lay in the past, but why two swords would be sufficient in that case is not clear. It seems likely, however, that the ironic interpretation so beloved by modern scholars, which would see the response of the apostles as a tragic misunderstanding, is anachronistic.

ARREST AND TRIAL

Luke continues to draw on Mark as his major source, but he revises freely. Instead of having Jesus go to the garden of Gethsemane, traditionally located in the Kidron valley at the bottom of the Mount of Olives, just down Mount Zion from the Temple precincts, Luke has him go to an undesignated place on the Mount of Olives (22:39). This was undoubtedly Jesus' regular lodging place during his stay in Jerusalem, as previously mentioned (21:37). Since his prediction of Peter's denial was made at the supper, there is no need to interrupt the narrative flow here to tell of it.

Luke's Jesus is much more in control than Mark's Jesus. In the calmness with which he faces death, it is plain that he is a model for potential martyrs in Luke's church. Indeed, he tells his disciples to pray that they enter not into temptation. Instead of falling to the ground, he calmly kneels. An angel comes to strengthen him, just as the martyr in Luke's time might expect to be strengthened. Even though Jesus was in "agony" and his sweat fell *like* drops of blood (which is not to say that it *was* drops of blood), it should not be thought that this was the eschatological struggle depicted in Mark. It was rather, to use the words of Robert Karris, "like the anguish of a weight lifter trying to lift five hundred pounds." Jesus is preparing himself for the ordeal ahead, so that he will be able to perform the Father's will.

Unlike Mark, Luke does not tell of Jesus' returning three times to discover the disciples asleep, unable to watch with him one hour. Instead, he returns only once, and their sleep is attributed to their sorrow. It is reminiscent of their sleep on the mount of transfiguration (9:32). They are to pray that they enter not into temptation. Again the command to watch and pray is one that has been relayed by Jesus to Luke's church as it waits out the second coming.

The story of the arrest also has characteristic Lukan alterations of the tradition received from Mark. The writing is much more concise and the narration is more direct. Judas comes to the place he knew Jesus stayed on the Mount of Olives, leading a crowd, the composition of which is not specified at first. Judas makes a move as if to kiss Jesus, although the identification of this as the signal of whom to arrest is not as explicit in Luke as it is in Mark. But Luke does report Jesus' poignant response to his erstwhile intimate follower, who can now be described as "the man called Judas." Jesus asks if the very sign of intimacy will also be the sign of betrayal. Only Luke tells us that the disciples, seeing what was about to happen, asked permission before they drew their swords—even if they did not wait for it before they used them. Again, only Luke tells us that when the right ear of the slave of the high priest was cut off, Jesus healed the ear, calling for an end to the violence and showing that he was not a revolutionary but a man of peace.

Not until then are those who had come out to arrest Jesus identified. They are not a mob dispatched by the religious authorities; the authorities are present in person, including the head of the Temple guard (22:52). Jesus' question why they did not try to arrest him while he was teaching daily in the Temple thus takes on a particular pointedness. They have come out as against a robber, which at that time generally meant a Zealot serving in a guerrilla band that sought to expel the Romans. All the way through, *Luke is careful to show that the Romans did not consider Jesus guilty of any crime.* Jesus' opponents have hidden their shameful deed under the cloak of darkness, and it is the hour of the powers of darkness (22:53).

Luke's narrative skill brings simplicity and movement into yet another scene (22:54–71). Peter's denial occurs prior to the trial before the Sanhedrin, so that Jesus must wait in the courtyard with his guards while Peter tries to blend into the crowd. This arrangement not only acknowledges the probability that the Sanhedrin did not meet at night, but also makes it possible for Jesus to look directly at Peter at the moment of the third denial, reminding him that Jesus had known he would behave like that. No wonder Peter went out and wept bitterly. Yet at least the reader is reminded that Jesus had described this denial as if Peter were being sifted by Satan like wheat (22:31–32). Even in the denial Jesus' prayer has been answered and Peter has not really failed; he will turn again and strengthen his brothers. Thus the denial is not the fall from grace in Luke that it is in Mark, nor does it have the vehemence (Mark 14:71). This is in line with Luke's tendency to be far less critical of the disciples than Mark, a tendency shown in the previous story, where they fell asleep only once while Jesus was praying in agony, and then from sorrow. For Mark's very different attitude and an explanation of it, see the companion volume to this, Werner Kelber's *Mark's Story of Jesus* (Philadelphia: Fortress Press, 1979).

At daybreak Jesus was led away to be tried before the council. "Sanhedrin" is the English rendering of the Aramaic transliteration of *sunedrion*, a Greek word for "council." The process has been greatly compressed so that it focuses on the one issue of Jesus' identity and the inability of the religious leaders to recognize it. We hear nothing about false witnesses here, nor about Jesus' having said, "I will destroy this Temple that is made with hands, and in three days I will build another, not made with hands" (Mark 14:58). The issue is exclusively christological: "If you are the Christ, tell us." Three terms are treated as synonymous: Christ (Messiah), Son of man, and Son of God. Indeed, a fourth is implied shortly before, when the guards call on Jesus to prophesy and say which one of them struck him; the Messiah is also the prophet like Moses. If one were to look only at these verses it could appear as if Luke did not apply these titles to Jesus, since they came only from his opponents and he neither affirms nor denies them, saying only "You say that I am." Yet the slightest familiarity with the rest of the gospel makes it clear that the issue here is not who Jesus is but the ability of his judges to take seriously what should have been obvious all along. This is shown in the way that Jesus' response is (a) taken by his opponents as an admission, and (b) thus all the evidence they need to convict him. Since they refuse to recognize the possibility that he might be who he says he is, his saying it can only be understood as blasphemy.

Luke constructed the scene of Jesus before Pilate (23:1–25) especially to show that Jesus was guilty of no crime against the Romans. This theme of the apolitical nature of the Christian movement and its civic righteousness will recur often in Acts, especially in the treatment of Paul. It is obvious that the author is anxious to defend the church in his own time against the charge of subversiveness. Here Luke has Pilate, the voice of Roman justice, proclaim three times that there is no evidence to suggest that Jesus has done anything to deserve the death penalty. He has to make that affirmation over the protest of the leaders of the Jewish people. Luke's purpose was not anti-Semitic in the sense that he had a vindictive attitude toward the Jewish people (an un-Christian attitude that most of Christ's followers through the centuries have had), but was rather pro-Christian, trying to help the Romans recognize that the church offered no political threat to the empire.

The charges made against Jesus by the leaders were patently false. That is, the charge that he forbade the payment of taxes to Caesar (23:2) is explicitly disproved by 20:25. When Pilate asks Jesus if he is a king, Jesus' reply, "You have said so," is very similar to the replies made to the Sanhedrin about the messiahship, but Pilate appears to take it as a denial, while the religious leaders took it as an admission. If it is at all legitimate to ask about the understanding of Jesus in this case or, better, Luke's implied understanding of the intention of Jesus, it would be: "I am a king, but not in any sense that should disturb Rome."

Luke makes a brilliant transition in 23:5 when he has the leaders accuse Jesus of stirring up people from Galilee to Judea, thus enabling Pilate to shift a difficult case to another court. Many scholars have pointed out that Herod appears in all three sections of Luke, but they have usually neglected to point out that there is no consistency in the portrayal. During the Galilean ministry he is curious about the identity of Jesus, in the travel narrative he seeks to kill him, and here he is only a sensation-seeker who would like to see a miracle. Again, it has been pointed out that this incident could be understood as a fulfillment of Ps. 2:2: "The kings of the earth set themselves, and the rulers take counsel together, against the Lord and his anointed." But since the counsel taken by Pilate and Herod is not *against* Jesus, and since Luke gives no indication that he has this passage in mind, the thesis seems unlikely. It also appears that nothing can be gained by seeking an allusion here to the biblically assumed reliability of the testimony of three witnesses. Perhaps the major accomplishment of Luke's bringing in Herod is that his soldiers rather than Roman soldiers mock Jesus and dress him in royal apparel.

The final irony becomes explicit in the last verse of the section: "[Pilate] released the man who had been thrown into prison for insurrection and for murder, whom they asked for; but Jesus he delivered up to their will" (23:25). The one innocent of crime against Rome was executed and the guilty one was set free.

All along Luke has excluded the people from the blame he laid on the leaders for rejecting Jesus. In 23:13, however, the people were finally brought into complicity. The full Lukan perspective on the role of the people in Jesus' death will be expressed in the speeches in Acts:

> Let all the house of Israel . . . know assuredly that God has made him both Lord and Christ, this Jesus whom you crucified. (Acts 2:36)

> . . . Jesus, whom you delivered up and denied in the presence of Pilate, when he had decided to release him. (3:13)

> But you denied the Holy and Righteous One, and asked for a murderer to be granted to you, and killed the Author of life, whom God raised from the dead. (3:14–15)

> And now, brethren, I know that you acted in ignorance, as did also your rulers. But what God foretold by the mouth of all the prophets, that his Christ should suffer, he thus fulfilled. (3:17–18)

It was from among these people that the women who followed Jesus to the cross emerged bewailing and lamenting. The paradox of their compassion and their complicity is allowed to stand. When they wept for him, however, Jesus said that they should weep instead for the destruction that was coming upon Jerusalem as a result of their denial of him before Pilate.

THE PROPHESIED DEATH OF THE MESSIAH

Luke's account of the crucifixion differs from Mark's account in a number of ways that suggest Luke's characteristic emphases rather than an additional source as the explanation. The theme of ready forgiveness for sins that appeared in the parable of the customs collector and the Pharisee and in the Zacchaeus episode recurs here—twice if we include verse 34, "Father, forgive them; for they know not what they do," which is missing from a number of important manuscripts. Since the idea of Jesus' forgiving his executioners seems so much in character for Jesus and so close to Lukan themes, it is hard to question the authenticity of the verse. Compare especially Stephen's similar words in Acts 7:60, a scene that Luke obviously modeled on the crucifixion; see also the theme of the ignorance of the Jews as an extenuating circumstance in their guilt for the death of Jesus in various speeches in Acts. These, incidentally, make it likely that Jesus' prayer included all involved in his death, Jews as well as Roman soldiers.

The passion narrative in Luke, as in the other Synoptics, echoes the language of Psalms 22 and 69, as well as that of Isaiah 53. Luke distinguishes between the participation in the crucifixion of the people, who were onlookers, and the participation of the leaders, who ridiculed Jesus. Along with "Christ of God," the leaders refer to Jesus derisively as "the elect one," a title that probably connects the Messiah with the chosen people but which is used of Jesus by only Luke in the Synoptics. A different form of the word appears in the transfiguration scene (9:35). The drink brought to Jesus by the soldiers is the vinegary wine they drank rather than the anesthetic variety mentioned by Mark. The Greek for the superscription is more emphatic in Luke than it is in the parallels: "*This* is the king of the Jews."

Only Luke tells of the penitent criminal. Without raising the question of whether Luke drew on an additional source of information it can be observed that he treats the two criminals as examples of two kinds of response to Jesus. The one joins in the mocking of the executioners, but the other recognizes that they have been condemned justly while Jesus' condemnation was unjust. With this exemplary use of the criminal in mind, it is irrelevant to speculate about his motives—for instance, whether he really believed that Jesus would come into his kingly power, or whether he was just humoring an unfortunate soul (probably a modern, psychologizing interpretation). By the same token, one cannot be too sure of the meaning of "today" and "paradise." Paradise was a Persian word for "garden" which was used in the Old Testament to refer to Eden and which came to be used in reference to the future state of the blessed. "Today" could have meant within twenty-four hours or it could have been intended as an eschatological reference to the new age that Jesus inaugurated. The real message is that the full blessings of forgiveness here and hereafter are available to those who repent.

Compared to the account in Mark, Luke's crucifixion story is almost tranquil, lacking any indication that Jesus felt forsaken by God or even that he was thirsty. Instead, in complete control of himself, he committed his spirit to his Father and expired. Further, the centurion in charge of the execution party made no christological confession that Jesus was the Son of God, as he did in Mark 15:39, but rather declared Jesus innocent, thus joining in the Roman exculpation of Jesus in which Luke was so interested. Jesus' followers, male and female, did not forsake him entirely, but stood and watched the proceedings from a safe distance so that in Acts they would be able to bear witness that Jesus fulfilled all the prophecies about how the Messiah should suffer.

HE IS RISEN

Luke adds little to Mark's account of the burial of Jesus beyond saying that Joseph of Arimathea did not consent to the decision of the Sanhedrin to crucify Jesus and that the women followers of Jesus knew where to find his tomb on Easter because they had followed Joseph when he took the body. When the women went to anoint Jesus' body for burial, they did not understand why the tomb was open and empty. The two angels, described as men in dazzling apparel, asked them why they sought the living among the dead and reminded them that Jesus' passion predictions, which he had begun to make in Galilee, also included a prediction of the resurrection. Part of Jesus' identity as a prophet all along had been his ability to forecast the future accurately, but here he is connected explicitly with the succession of prophets who had predicted the execution and resurrection of the Messiah.

When the women reported this wonderful news to the Eleven, they were not taken seriously. This is probably not so much a historical reminiscence as it is a narrative device to prolong the suspense so the story can reach a climax and end with Jesus' reunion with the disciples. Many modern translations omit verse 12, "But Peter arose and ran to the tomb; stooping and looking in, he saw the linen cloths by themselves; and he went home wondering at what had happened." It is not included in many ancient manuscripts, but the best ones do contain it. Further, it could have been this outing on which Jesus appeared to Peter (12:34). All in all, the arguments for accepting the verse as genuine seem stronger than those against doing so.

The source to which the Emmaus episode (24:13–35) is usually attributed is Luke (L). The essential truth of that attribution is negative: Luke did not get the story from either Mark or Q, neither of which had any resurrection-appearance stories. To affirm positively, on the other hand, that this narrative existed prior to the composition of Luke's gospel in some tradition, oral or written, is not only to go beyond the evidence but also to be beyond probability. Precisely because it is such a good story it bears all the marks of Lukan composition. Beyond that, its theological purposes are plain.

Indeed, similar things might be said about all resurrection-appearance stories, changing only the name of the evangelist to whom each is attributed, since it is impossible to harmonize any set of them into a coherent succession of transmission. Each of the stories does, however, have the same sequence of elements:

1. The situation

2. The appearance of the Lord

3. The greeting

4. The recognition

5. The word of command

Only the word of command is lacking here, being reserved for the appearance to the whole group of disciples in verses 48–49.

As in the other resurrection-appearance stories, Jesus is not recognized when he first joins two of his loquacious followers who were on the road to Emmaus. This lack of recognition is not to be ascribed entirely to their lack of expectation. There seems to be both continuity and discontinuity between the resurrected body and the body that hung upon the cross: Jesus could show his hands and feet and even eat a piece of fish, but he could also appear and disappear suddenly. Then, too, the recognition is one of the elements of a resurrection-appearance story, which indicates that the risen Lord was assumed to look somehow different from the way he had looked before.

As moving as the story is, its contrived character shows between the seams. For instance, it is hard to believe that any of the disciples could have left Jerusalem after the empty tomb had been reported and the women had repeated the angels' message. Surely no follower of Jesus could have left town before the mystery was cleared up, except for some emergency—and none is mentioned. The whole story is obviously designed to have Jesus go through all the Scriptures, "beginning with Moses and all the prophets," to show that it was "necessary that the Christ should suffer these things and enter into his glory" (24:26). The verb meaning "to be necessary" is the same one that has been used all along to indicate that what Jesus did was in fulfillment of God's plan of salvation which had been revealed through the prophets of the Old Testament.

Even when Jesus had expounded the Scriptures, the disciples going to Emmaus did not recognize him. It was not until they stopped for the night and he said the table blessing that they knew who he was, even though they later recalled that their hearts had burned within them as he had interpreted the Scriptures to them along the road. The message is clear: It was in the Eucharist that the early church was aware of the presence of its risen Lord.

After they recognized Jesus, the disciples rushed back to Jerusalem to tell everyone there what had happened to them. When they arrived they received the word that Jesus had also appeared to Peter, called by his Hebrew name Simon. The patched quality of the transition from one story to the other is visible when, after the news of two resurrection appearances has been reported to them, the disciples are still "startled and frightened" by Jesus' presence with them because they think he is a ghost (a better translation than the RSV's "spirit").

Luke makes certain that his readers know the resurrection body was not just a phantom by having Jesus both show his tangible hands and feet and also eat some food, something a ghost was

incapable of doing (compare John 21:13). Then Jesus repeats his
proof that everything he had done had been prophesied in the
Old Testament, referring to "the law of Moses, and the prophets,
and the psalms," thus alluding to all three divisions of the Hebrew canon.

Moving from his death and resurrection, which had just occurred, Jesus goes on to talk about the equally prophesied result of
those events, namely, that "repentance and forgiveness of sins
should be preached in his name to all nations." This will be the
subject of the Book of Acts, after the disciples receive the Pentecost gift of "power from on high" (Acts 2:1–4). When they have
received the Holy Spirit, the disciples will be "witnesses" to Jesus
"in Jerusalem and in all Judea and Samaria and to the end of the
earth" (Acts 1:8).

The resurrection-appearance traditions implied in Mark and explicit in Matthew and John 21 all suggest that Jesus appeared to the
Twelve in Galilee, but it is plain that Luke kept the action in
Jerusalem so that the story could be picked up there in the Book of
Acts. Because Luke counted on having both volumes read, and not
the gospel alone, any interpretation of just the gospel will have an
incomplete quality; one waits, if not for the other shoe to be
dropped, at least for the chord to be resolved.

Still, there is a break between the two volumes, and the gospel
needs an ascension story on which to close, even though the fuller
report of that event will be reserved for the next volume. Thus we
have a short account tacked on here. It has puzzled many genera-
tions of interpreters, including the scribes who copied many of our
manuscripts and left out the words "and was carried up into
heaven" because they assumed that Luke could not have intended
to report the ascension here since he knew perfectly well that it
occurred forty days later and in the next installment. The disciples
then returned to Jerusalem and the Temple where the gospel began
and where Acts will pick up the story. Acts, however, will tell how
the Spirit-filled community moved out from there to Rome, the
center of the earth. The story, then, is

to be continued.